UNIVERSITY OF NORTH CAROLINA
STUDIES IN THE ROMANCE LANGUAGES AND LITERATURES
Number 111

RELIGIOUS ELEMENTS IN THE SECULAR
LYRICS OF THE TROUBADOURS

RELIGIOUS ELEMENTS IN THE SECULAR LYRICS OF THE TROUBADOURS

BY

RAYMOND GAY-CROSIER

CHAPEL HILL
THE UNIVERSITY OF NORTH CAROLINA PRESS

For Ruth

DEPÓSITO LEGAL: V. 4.117 - 1971

ARTES GRÁFICAS SOLER, S. A. — JÁVEA, 28 — VALENCIA (8) — 1971

CONTENTS

			Pages
PREFACE			9
INTRODUCTION			11
CHAPTER	I.	HISTORICAL OUTLINE	13
—	II.	A SURVEY OF THEORIES CONCERNING ORIGINS	24
		1. The Folk-Song Theory	25
		2. The Arabic Theory	26
		3. The Classical Latin Theory	27
		4. The Medieval Latin Theory	28
		5. The Liturgical Theory	32
—	III.	THE TROUBADOURS' CONCEPTION OF LOVE	37
—	IV.	THE VOCABULARY OF "CORTEZIA"	44
		A) 1. *penedensaria*	44
		2. *pecat*	45
		3. *colpa*	46
		4. *merces*	47
		5. *almorna*	48
		6. *mana*	48
		7. *obediensa*	48
		8. *martir*	49
		B) 1. *mi dons*	50
		2. *pasio*	51
		3. *joy*	51
		4. *solatz*	53
		5. *deport*	54
		6. *deduch*	54
		C) 1. *pregar*	55
		2. *adorar*	55

			3.	*orar*	57
			4.	*batejar*	57
		D)	1.	*falhir*	57
			2.	*servir*	59
			3.	*guerir*	60
CHAPTER V.	THE THEMES OF "CORTEZIA"				63
		1.	Love as a civilizing power		63
		2.	The theme of mercy		65
		3.	The theme of joy		67
		4.	Praise of the lady		69
		5.	The theme of the Virgin Mary		72
		6.	The commandments of love		73
		7.	The beginnings of a true religion of love ...		76
		8.	Various themes of religious origin		82
		9.	The martyrdom of love		85
		10.	The possibilities of mystical influence		88
IN LIEU OF A CONCLUSION					99
BIBLIOGRAPHY					101

PREFACE

This study was originally composed in German. When the author took up a teaching post in Canada and later in the United States, it was considered more appropriate that it should be published in the language of those to whom it is particularly addressed. Professor Robert Taylor, who gives instruction in Old French and Old Porvençal at Victoria College, University of Toronto, was kind enough to prepare the English translation, as well as to offer a number of helpful suggestions concerning the content. For his patient effort I offer sincere thanks. My gratitude goes also to my colleague, Professor George Diller, who proposed several judicious ideas. I am grateful, too, for courtesies extended by my friend, Professor Frieda S. Brown, Michigan State University, who has greatly lightened the labor of editing the final stage of the manuscript. Its typing was made possible through a subsidy of the Graduate School of the University of Florida whose generous help I sincerely appreciate.

R. G.-C.

University of Florida, Fall 1968.

INTRODUCTION

The chief purpose of the present study is to explore the possible sphere of influence exercised by religious traditions on the origin and development of the lyrics of the troubadours. An examination of existing criticism reveals that Provençal scholars have, to date, been often partial in their approach. A balanced analysis is therefore necessary.

Throughout my text, I have preferred to emphasize the term *sphere of influence* rather than the traditional one of *source*, since the former implies the strict avoidance of any one rigid approach or point of view.

The study of influence and/or sources is a vast and complex problem which no single investigation, such as this one, could hope to solve. Thus, no attempt or claim is made to comprehensiveness. This discussion has instead been limited to the secular lyric. Marcabru is generally excluded, for example, as being too religiously oriented, but occasional references will be made to those of his passages which are secular in nature. On the other hand, in the effort to guard against narrowness of application, care has been taken to draw illustrative quotations wherever possible from a representative group of the best known troubadours (a practice which has not always been followed by recent scholars, e.g. Scheludko). In this way, it becomes even more clear that all of the most important themes of the *canso* may be traced back to the poems of Guillaume IX. No consideration is given to versification. Finally, I should like to emphasize the introductory character of the present study. It wants to clearly pose the problems involved rather than resolve them.

CHAPTER I

HISTORICAL OUTLINE

Even a perfunctory examination of the geographical and ethnological characteristics of southern and southwestern France and the neighbouring areas of eastern Spain can shed a good deal of light on the literature which grew up there. This whole area, but especially southern France, has benefited enormously from its particular geographical situation and from an almost organic mixture of the various races which came together there at one period or another.[1] It is generally believed that the prehistoric population was made up of three groups. The presence of the Ligurians may be traced back to the second millenium B.C.; the Celts are thought to have entered the area about 900-800 B.C., followed, about 600 B.C., by the Iberians migrating north from Africa. This postulated base population was not affected as was that of northern Gaul by the first onslaught of the pre-Christian migratory shifts. On the other hand, it was much more profoundly influenced than the north by the colonizing efforts of dominant cultures. The Romans were, of course, the most significant of these, but hardly less important for the "exotic" sphere of influence were the Greeks who established colonies in the area between 600 and 300 B.C. Even centuries after their withdrawal, traces of their enterprising spirit and artistic refinement were still evident in Marseilles, the center of the Greek

---

[1] Cf. Camproux, Charles, *Histoire de la littérature occitane*, p. 12: "carrefour des races."

colonial area. In later centuries the Arabic influence was added to the others.

Although the subsequent period of Germanic invasions affected the whole of Romania, the population of the south was again in a relatively favoured position, since it was settled mainly by the Visigoths, culturally the most advanced of the "barbarians." The geographical situation as well favoured the development of an autochthonous culture. The south was cut off from the north by mountain ranges and rivers, which in the earlier periods represented almost impassable barriers to communication. The gates of Provence opened instead in quite different directions—toward Spain, Italy and the Near East. Kiener speaks appropriately of the "reflection of the way of life and patterns of thought of the ancients." [2] His remark is confirmed most obviously in the realm of architectural art. The church of St.-Trophime in Arles, for example, shows a conscious acceptance of classical attitudes and structural principles.

The Orient, too, as it was experienced by the Crusaders and the merchants, played an important rôle as a potential source of inspiration. In his very well-informed study on *Amour Courtois et Fin'Amors dans la littérature du XIIe siècle*,[3] Moshé Lazar points out that the discovery of the oriental world liberated the creative imagination of the writers and artisans of southern France.

> [L']importation de produits de luxe et de valeurs spirituelles allait favoriser l'éveil et le développement d'un mouvement social que l'on pourrait qualifier "laïque" ou "profane," s'orientant dans un sens contraire au courant ascétique et réformiste des clunisiens et des cisterciens. Elle allait alimenter par la suite une nouvelle génération d'écrivains et d'artistes, et faire éclore, en marge de l'église, "un humanisme courtois." [4]

---

[2] Kiener, *Verfassungsgeschichte der Provence*, Leipzig 1900, quoted after Kinkel, Hans, "Die kulturellen Grundlagen der provenzalischen Trobadordichtung" in *Archiv für das Studium der neueren Sprachen und Literaturen*, 1909, p. 334; a few of Kiener's precisely formulated results are incorporated into this outline.

[3] Paris, 1964.

[4] *Ibid.*, p. 10; the expression "humanisme courtois" is taken from Jean Frappier's *Le Roman Breton*, Paris, 1951.

The southern region was characterized, in very general terms, by the development of a culture stressing social behaviour and the art of living, rather than one which was predominantly intellectual, as in the north. The proliferation of well-known monastic and episcopal schools in the north had no counterpart in the south; particularly lacking were schools firmly rooted in historically significant tradition. Only Montpellier, the university centre for the Catalan-Aragon region, has risen to a position of influence, and it was sold to the French king in 1349. The diocese centres of Poitiers and Angoulême, the abbeys of St. Cyprien and St. Victor de Marseille as well as the later important St. Martial, all achieved fame only during the eleventh and twelfth centuries. Kinkel points out, however, that these facts would not allow us to conclude that there was any lack of normal education. "Did not monastic schools attain their maximum stature in areas where they were struggling against barbarism? Would not the opposite conclusion be more justified then: that in fact the lack of outstanding schools (not the lack of schools in general) may be taken as an indication of a relatively high cultural level, which did not call for outstanding counter-measures on the part of the schools, and which in fact prevented their vigorous growth?"[5] This is an interesting point of view, but it must be borne in mind that the only real centres of learning in the south were found among the fragmented and divided ranks of the aristocratic classes, which were forced to develop into a feudal structure as a form of protection against the enemy. In fact, it would not be unreasonable to claim that the top levels of society retained a monopoly on education until the rise of the bourgeoisie.

This line of thought leads directly to a tempting hypothesis, one which can best be confirmed by an examination of the troubadour lyrics themselves, even though their testimony may occasionally be ambiguous. It has been assumed that a secular tradition in education developed over a period of about three hundred years (the ninth to twelfth centuries) in the south, standing, to our eyes at least, diametrically opposed to the religious tradition of the north. This particular orientation provided rich

---

[5] Kinkel, *op. cit.*, p. 335.

and fertile ground for the development of secular poetry. However, it must be mentioned at the outset that the adjectives "secular" and "religious" are in fact not entirely appropriate terms, since they suggest an absolute division. The notion of "syncretism," as we shall see later, would correspond more precisely to the actual situation. For there arose at a very early period an "eloquentia christiana," defined by E. Gilson as "éloquence étendue au sens de Cicerón, mais où la sagesse chrétienne remplaçait celle des philosophes." The secular lyrics of the troubadours are therefore inconceivable apart from the religious traditions out of which they sprang, just as religious literature could not develop into poetry except by its union with secular lyricism.

The cultural rise of the south coincided with the full development of feudalism, which may be placed between 887 (dethronement of Charles the Fat) and 1180 (death of Louis VII). Feudalism formed the sociological framework for the poet-knights, and before long non-aristocratic poets were welcomed to the same circles, as long as they were skilled in the use of panegyric. Finally there developed a general tendency toward an "aristocracy of the mind." The severely standardized patterns of thought characteristic of feudal structures (often more theoretical than real in the south), certainly had their influence on the poetry, but this factor ought not to be exaggerated, as has been the case from time to time.

The political situation in southern France became the real test of feudalism. The chief reason for the swift formation and development of the feudal system was the continuing series of conflicts with the Saracens. But civil disturbances and confusion — there was no sign of a strong monarchy — were also responsible to a large degree for the clarification and confirmation of the relationships between lord and vassal in which land was exchanged for military service. A scattered realm had developed — a "partnership of free aristocrats" [6] — without any central power, held together by thousands of agreements between independent individuals. These individuals felt strong enough, even

---

[6] *Ibid.*, p. 338.

vis-à-vis the Church, to engage in a rather confused pattern of local politics and to take pleasure in a very subjectively-oriented poetry, which sometimes went as far as obscenity and blasphemy. The best-known representative of this type of society was Guillaume IX of Aquitaine. The Provençal princes had an Augustinian concept of the state in which the Church was to limit itself to matters of the soul, leaving earthly concerns entirely to the state. This attitude was to be strongly challenged, especially in the thirteenth century, by the new development of the Papacy, which was supported for political reasons by the French king. The relatively weak position of the Church as compared to its status in the north was perhaps also due in part to the fact that the episcopate was made up largely of relatives of the landed nobility, as a result of the attitude which considered church offices as a convenient means of providing for problematical cases of legacy. The higher clergy was secularized before it even entered upon its functions.

At the beginning of the eleventh century, the southern regions of France were controlled by four main sovereign powers: the Duchies of Aquitaine, Gascony, Toulouse and Barcelona. These may be considered as small but independent kingdoms, since the power of the king was here only a nominal one without political significance. The court of Alphonse II, one of the most influential of the period, sheltered Guiraut de Bornelh, Raimbaut d'Orange, Folque de Marseille, Peire Vidal, Peire Rogier, Peire Raimon de Toulouse, Uc Brunet, Arnaut Daniel, lo Monge de Montaudon, Pons de Capduelh, Raimbaut de Vaqueiras, and perhaps Aimeric de Sarlat. It was out of this social framework, in which the individual man displayed and was, in fact, obliged to display a pronounced self-consciousness, that secular poetry developed. In order to understand it, we must first consider briefly two central concepts which are mutually influential and complementary — the place of the lady, and the conception of *cortezia* together with all related notions.

The man of the Midi is on the whole characterized by a strong tendency toward individualism. Of course such a generalization is inevitably superficial, but it should be understood that our purpose is not to define racial characteristics but rather to set forth *one* of many possible explanations for the rise of secular poetry. Even the Romans spoke in praise of the *cothurnus gallicanus* of Aquitaine as opposed to the *gravitas romana* of Provincia.

> Le midi joua dans cette évolution des esprits un rôle de catalyseur et de diffuseur. L'Eglise y avait été de tous temps moins sévère et moins active aussi que dans le Nord de la France. L'emprise des clercs sur les classes possédantes etait quasi nulle, et celles-ci purent développer librement une *idéologie amoureuse, une morale profane,* une joie de vivre (nettement en contradiction avec l'enseignement chrétien) dont il nous sera aisé de retrouver le reflet dans la lyrique des troubadours. [7]

The tendency to look down on the common masses may be seen as well in the trend toward *trobar clus,* in which the troubador stresses his individuality to the point of becoming incomprehensible.

Nevertheless, even the representatives of a less hermetic style took some pains to veil their personalities in their poetic works. This may be illustrated by the typical sketches that Jean Frappier gives of four well-known poets of the time; his description may be applied equally well to the poetry or to the poets themselves. Guillaume de Poitiers stands out for his "fougue mêlée de gaillardise"; Jaufré Rudel, the poet of *amor de lonh,* for his "mélancolie raffinée"; Marcabru, whose treatment of the theme of love is quite opposed to the generally accepted concepts, for his "vigueur et violence satirique"; and Bernart de Ventador, who glorified the notion of *joi,* for his "ardeur passionnée." [8]

The development of a temporal, courtly culture has already been mentioned, representing a certain contrast to spiritual culture. As is always the case with opposites, these had a fruitful effect on one another and acted as stimulants in the state of tension arising between the temporal and spiritual traditions. To be sure, the latter borrowed more from the former, but it is well known that the so-called spiritual tradition sprang from a still older

---

[7] Lazar, *op. cit.,* pp. 10-11; I underline.

[8] Frappier, Jean, "Vues sur les conceptions courtoises dans les littératures d'oc et d'oïl du douzième siècle," *Cahiers de Civilisation Médiévale,* II, 1959, p. 138.

temporal one. Secular poetry is in no way a creation *ex nihilo*, nor is it the spontaneous product of an enthusiastic folk-consciousness, as the Romantic school of philologists was determined to believe. Instead, both of these traditions are to be seen as Renaissances with the balance of their relative importance changing from one to the other in the course of time. Each tradition stands on such a complex base that several theories concerning origins have been postulated, as we shall see. Certainly secular poetry was able to draw upon the accumulated knowledge of the centuries, to which it gave new life and breadth under the social conditions which have been outlined. The original element in this poetry, the *religion of love*, is itself inconceivable except in relation to its spiritual model. It corresponds to the orthodox Aristotelian concept of art as *imitatio*. The real contribution of the troubadours lies in the consistent transposition of religious categories of thought into the realm of the glorification of woman. G. Cohen shows a fine sense of psychological observation in his remark that:

> S'il est une doctrine, s'il est un sentiment que l'on peut à bon droit attribuer à la France, à la France méridionale surtout, c'est la déification de la femme dans la poésie. [...] Il n'est donc pas si surprenant que, d'ordre du destin ou de la Providence, il ait appartenu au tempérament français d'élever en dignité la femme, d'en faire non pas seulement la source de toute beauté, mais l'incarnation de toutes les vertus et l'inspiration de toute vaillance.... Dans quelle mesure le christianisme eut-il part à cette innovation spirituelle [...] il est d'autant plus malaisé de le dire que le culte de Notre-Dame fut lui-même influencé, du moins dans sa forme, et peut-être développé par la doctrine de l'amour courtois. En vérité il en est de ce problème comme de celui de l'origine du langage, il faut renoncer à le poursuivre jusque dans ses extrêmes limites. Nous allons jusqu'à la source, nous la voyons jaillir du sol; il est vain de creuser la terre pour retrouver le trajet des gouttelettes qui l'ont formée.[9]

Inseparably linked with the central status of woman, the courtly ideal consisted of a number of social refinements which grew out of it. These refinements, designated collectively by the

---

[9] Cohen, Gustave, *Chrétien de Troyes et son œuvre*, Paris², 1948, p. 34 sq.

term *cortezia*, were an essential part of the moral code of the true courtier and lover. The Old Provençal *cort* (eleventh century) is derived from the Vulgar Latin *curtis* (Classical *cohors*, courtyard, influenced by *curia*). Even in Classical Latin *cohors* had the meaning "retinue of a prince," from which it is only a small semantic step to "entourage of a court." Later the semantic field was even further broadened. From the twelfth century on, *court* is used in Old French for the meaning of "court of justice." The adjective derived from *cort* is *cortes* in Old Provençal, meaning "having to do with the court, courtly, well-bred, pleasing." The corresponding abstract noun is *cortezia*.

The courtly ideal is a social, literary and moral phenomenon. Even the most self-possessed of the nobility, for whom the Church represented a political rather than a moral institution, felt the need of an ethical foundation for their way of life. Along with the poets, and in fact often in the forefront, the aristocracy helped to develop the courtly ideal, a moral code which was both the expression and the goal of the "nouveau style de vie. La réalité historique a suscité un besoin d'expression, un miroir où elle put se refléter." [10] The formulation of a social existence was indispensable even for the most determined of individualists. The courtly ideal in the south was an attempt at this socialization in distinctly secular terms. In the north the knight strove more often to attain the position of a *miles Christi*, for which he had to abandon all the courtly conventions which would keep him from his lofty goal. Love was generall represented in the "chanson de geste" as an effeminate emotion. It was necessarily subordinated to chivalrous deeds and was thought of as a minor source of virtue in relation to the divine quest — a view which clearly anticipates the Cornelian concept of love. Not so, however, in the south. Love was the most elevated feeling a knight or lover could hope to attain, and, indeed, it was recognized as an essential part of true masculinity. The goal was to become a *miles cythereus* or *chevalier amoureux*. For the knight of Ille-de-France, *amour courtois* [11] meant simply "le raffinement extrême de la courtoisie," without implying the

---

[10] Frappier, *op. cit.*, p. 135.
[11] Frappier, *op. cit.*, p. 136.

attainment of *courtoisie* itself. The Provençal lover recognized in this conception of love a social and moral value, which he called not *amour courtois* — a word of recent coinage — but *veraï amors, bon'amors, fin'amors.*

In this connection it is worthwhile to mention a recent article by Ruprecht Rohr, "Zur Skala der ritterlichen Tugenden in der altprovenzalischen und altfranzösichen höfischen Dichtung," preceded by this remark of Curtius concerning the chivalric system of virtues: "The so-called system of virtues of the knight was probably never really a system. It contained ethical and aesthetic elements of a secular nature, many of which had been developed long before the establishment of chivalry." [12] Rohr draws our attention to the predilection for a grouping of notions by twos or by threes, such as *joven-amor-joi, joi-amor, cortezia-joi-deport, servir-sofrir,* etc. For Rohr love is "the last rung of the ladder which leads directly to God," and he presents the ladder as follows:

Virtues
{
Dieu
Amor
Proeza
Joven
Cortezia
Vergonha, Mezura
Ensenhamen
}

Poestat — Savieza — Aver   may be considered as vices or virtues

Vices
{
Follatura
Putia — Orguelh — Desmezura
Vilania
Malvestat
Aman Malvolensa [13]
}

Two of these subcategories of *cortezia* are worth examining briefly in a little more detail: *mezura* is a collective term for "savoir-vivre, humility, self-control, a balance between emotion

---

[12] Curtius, Ernst Robert, *Europäische Literatur und lateinisches Mittelalter,* Berne³, 1961, p. 520.

[13] Rohr, Ruprecht, *op. cit., Zeitschrift für Romanische Philologie,* 78, 1962, p. 305.

and reason"; *joven* means, according to Frappier, "disponibilité spontanée (this term may now, of course, be too heavily fraught with other implications because of its association with Gide) sans arrière-pensée ni calcul, à se montrer généreux, à distribuer les dons magnifiques et à savoir bien courtiser les dames (bien domnejar)." [14] Only those who have attained these qualities are *cortes*, worthy of the courtly milieu and qualified for the service of love. *Cortezia*, therefore, is a term embodying a whole series of the most admirable of qualities and representing the achievement of perfect equilibrium, absolute self-control, flawless social and moral behaviour.

Marcabru's central notion of *fin'amor* represents not only the dogma and ritual of serious love but corresponds also to a true concern of the heart which stems from the exaltation of a serious mind. For one thing it acts as a counterbalance to the widespread use of marriage for practical convenience or as a means of political alliance. Very quickly too, love came to be considered as something sacred, and the spiritual concept was given form through artistic skill. As part of this movement, there were more and more direct borrowings of religious themes to emphasize the value of earthly love. But, as Jean Frappier justly points out: "le 'fin'amor' ne reste pas moins associé au désir charnel, tantôt voilé par des euphémismes, des périphrases et des métaphores, tantôt crûment avoué." [15]

Prudence is necessary in the search for Platonic influences. Especially with Jaufré Rudel the temptation is great to postulate Plato and Plotinus as sources of his *amor de lonh*. It may after all be true to a certain extent that these philosophers did originate the idea of distant love, but the poets were never conscious of this. "La fréquence de l'imagerie érotique dans les chansons de [Jaufré Rudel] suffit à écarter ce genre d'interprétation. On peut dire tout au plus que son inassouvissement amoureux se réfugie dans le rêve sans se diluer ou se transformer en un mysticisme proprement religieux." [16] But mysticism does not need to be exclusively religious; we shall come back to this point later. The

---

[14] Frappier, *op. cit.*, p. 139.
[15] Frappier, *op. cit.*, p. 140.
[16] *Ibid.*

lady, then, played an important role in the refinement of the Provençal aristocracy. *Cortezia* became a real force, a means of trying to check the almost unimaginable brutality which was the lot of women. The tendency toward sublimation did not mean however that secular love was suddenly spiritualized. More accurately, it was refined to fit the courtly milieu and played, in varying degrees, the part of a substitute for religion or moral behaviour, depending on the predominant conception of its nature. "Cette religion de l'amour constitue l'élaboration la plus audacieuse et la plus hérétique d'un paganisme mondain." [17] Before proceeding to a closer consideration of a few elements which were borrowed from religious traditions, it will be valuable to outline the various theories concerning origins and establish their relative significance.

---

[17] *Ibid.*, p. 143.

Chapter II

A SURVEY OF THEORIES CONCERNING ORIGINS

As has already been indicated, the study of themes and vocabulary leads back to the problem of sources, not only for philological considerations but for the needs of literary history as well. Scholars have in the past been all too eager to cry Eureka on the basis of a few scattered examples or, even more frequently, on the basis of an unscientific prejudice. It must be confessed that at the present time the final solution to the problem of origins seems almost as far off as it ever was. In fact if we reflect even superficially on the extreme complexity of the question, we are inclined to agree with Cohen's remark concerning the prime source: "Il est vain de creuser la terre pour retrouver le trajet des gouttelettes qui l'ont formée [i.e. the source]."

A number of illustrious scholars thought otherwise, and there are still those who maintain their a priori attitude even today. A great number of theories have been formulated, many of them quite convincing in themselves, but most of them suffer from the same weakness: they are one-sided because of the tendency to draw absolute conclusions from the results of a limited field of research. The theories fall generally into one of five main groups. The most tenacious has undoubtedly been the folk-song theory, which was accepted throughout Europe in conjunction with the Romantic movement. The Arabic theory was developed at about the same time but was pushed into the background until modern times when it has experienced a strong revival. The Classical Latin, Medieval Latin and Liturgical theories represent still an inexhaustible reservoir which can provide the modern scholar with research material for many years to come.

1. *The Folk-Song Theory*

One of the most important propagators of the notion that "l'ignorance créatrice" was the origin of all true poetry was Johann Gottfried Herder. A passage from his *Vorrede der Volkslieder* indicates better than a lengthy discussion why the theory of popular origins was so widely acclaimed and why it has in fact lost none of its convincing power even today for a few die-hard followers:

> Montaigne says: "Folk poetry, being entirely a part of nature, is so naive and charming as to equal the classical beauty of the most refined creations of artistic poetry...." There can surely be no doubt that *poetry* and particularly musical poetry was in the beginning quite like a *folk-song*, that is, light, simple, consisting of images and vocabulary belonging to the simple folk, just like the richness of nature itself, accessible to all. Singing needs crowds, the harmony of many voices; it demands the ear of the listener and the blending of heart and voice. If it had been an art form contracted of letters and syllables, or a visual representation stressing composition and colour, intended for an indolent reading public, then it would never have been created [troubadour poetry was made up precisely and almost entirely of these elements], or if created, it would never have developed into what it is now in all regions of the world. Every country and every language, especially the age-old, mysterious Orient, could furnish many traces of this origin, if it were necessary to demonstrate and enumerate them.... [Poetry] dwelt in the ear of the people, on the lips and on the harpstrings of living singers; it sang of history, adventure, mystery, wonder and omen; it was the full expression of the character of a people, of its language, its passions and its arrogance, its music and its soul.[1]

---

[1] *Herders Dichtungen, Stimmen der Völker in Liedern*, I, 224-225.

Whoever is capable of giving such eloquent expression to a theory is sure to find disciples. Jacob Grimm and Ludwig Uhland were Herder's intellectual heirs. The best-known representatives among Romance scholars were Friedrich Diez, who worked under the encouragement of Goethe and Schlegel, Claude Fauriel and the old masters, Gaston Paris and Joseph Bédier. Alfred Jeanroy also worked from the a priori assumption that folk poetry always preceded the artistic forms, even though Guillaume IX does not exactly illustrate this supposition. Later Paris and Jeanroy further developed their views through the May-Dance Theory, according to which the inspiration for Provençal lyrics was seen as originating in the courtly May Day celebrations. In Italy, A. Restori, in Germany, E. Wechssler, Suchier and Voretzsch show at least some traces of this Romantic theory. Menéndez Pidal attempted to reconcile the differences that separated folk and conscious poetry, characterizing them as "poesía popular" and "poesía tradicional" respectively.

2. *The Arabic Theory*

The Arabic theory is put here in second place in order to indicate that it belongs, along with the folk-song theory, to the group of hypotheses which are rather one-sided right from the outset. It too was developed out of the same wave of enthusiasm characteristic of Romanticism, which had a feeling for universal relationships and interconnections and was thus able to lay the foundations for Indo-European linguistics. The outstanding representatives of this tendency are: Herder, P. L. Guingené (*Histoire de la littérature d'Italie*, Paris, 1811), Chateaubriand (*Génie du christianisme, Etudes et discours historiques*), Josef Görres (*Altteusche Volks- und Meisterlieded*, Frankfurt, 1817), Claude Fauriel, who had shrewd reservations to make (*Histoire de la poésie provençale*, Paris, 1846), F. Villemain (*Tableau de la littérature du moyen-âge*, Paris, 1878). The latter had this to say: "La véritable similitude de la parenté de génie n'existe pour [la poésie provençale] qu'avec cette littérature de l'Orient, dont il faut vous parler, malgré mon ignorance... C'est par mille détours que le souffle de la poésie arabe, le parfum de l'Arabie est arrivé dans notre Occident... c'est par une transmission invisible, par une contagion poétique et populaire."[2] It must also be noted that the Arabic influence came by way of Spain where it was transformed into Mozarabic through fusion with Christian traditions. As early as 1775, Thomas Warton was exploring in these directions. In his *History of English Poetry* we find a passage which indicates perceptiveness, although he does not delve further into the problem: "...the Troubadours of Provence in great measure caught this turn of fabling from Spain." The abovementioned works must be read with caution, as Villemain himself advises with the words "malgré mon ignorance." The authors are by no means Arabic specialists and therefore do not always draw competent conclusions. In more recent times the Arabic theory has been revived. A series of true experts have undertaken thorough-going research, particularly in the area of themes and of versification. Ribera and Anglès, dealing with the music, and Nykl, Briffault, Menéndez Pidal, Dermenghem, Le Gentil and Davenson and many others, dealing with the texts, have produced results which at the very least make it impossible to reject entirely the theory of Arabic influence (cf. bibliogr.).

3. *The Classical Latin Theory*

The ramifications of the Latin Classical period went unnoticed by the Romantics. At the beginning of the present century, a few scholars favoured the Latin theory, partly as a reaction against the folk-song theory. Schlegel and Fauriel had already established certain parallels between some of the troubadours and Ovid. Willibald Schrötter (*Ovid und die Troubadours,* Halle, 1908) and Edmond Faral (*Recherches sur les sources latines des contes et romans courtois du Moyen Age,* Paris, 1913) investigated the problem more thoroughly. Many common themes were discovered, such as love instigated by nature, love as military service and many more. According to Stanislaus Stronski (*Le Troubadour Folquet de Marseille,* Krakau, 1910), Livy, Publius Syrius, Seneca,

---

[2] Villemain, *Tableau de Littérature du moyen-âge,* quoted after Axhausen, K., *Die Theorien über den Ursprung der provenzalischen Lyrik,* Marburg, 1937, p. 25.

Tacitus and Virgil also served as direct or indirect models. To be sure the troubadours remained on the surface, and did not penetrate into the real spirit of the Ancients.[3] Another name appears in this connection, which we shall have occasion to mention more than once in later sections: Dimitri Scheludko. This Rumanian scholar, who has specialized particularly in the religious sphere of influence, upholds the view that the Latin theory has more chance of success than the Arabic or folk-song theories.[4] Ovid's influence is not evident in the early troubadour poetry but is obviously present in Bernard de Ventadour, who must have read him.

The Classical Latin theory sees the troubadour lyrics as a conscious art form built upon a foundation rich with tradition. Just as in the Ovidian model, love, particularly in the later developments of the *canso*, becomes an art which may be acquired: the art of *gay saber*. It must not be overlooked that the points held in common by Antiquity and by the troubadours consist mostly of traditional maxims and images which belong to all literatures. Classical rhetoric also played a very important part in the transmission of the oldest of topoi. It is unfortunate that a Romance scholar of the rank of Vossler should simply dismiss this promising view in such strong terms: "These witty, adaptable, highly original Provençal poets [the adjectives are exaggerated purposely] are transformed by such investigations of sources into stupid, dull, insensitive and unoriginal blokheads."[5] There can be no question of "blockheads" unless the rich tradition of themes becomes nothing more than the mere foundation without a new and independent structure, which of course is not the case for the best of the troubadours.

4. *The Medieval Latin Theory*

Although the demonstration of an indirect influence from Latin antiquity is made difficult, because conclusions can at best be

---

[3] See Axhausen, *op. cit.*, p. 40.
[4] Scheludko, "Die klassisch-lateinische Theorie," *Archivum Romanicum*, II, 1927, pp. 271-312.
[5] Vossler, K., review of Schrötter, quoted after Axhausen, p. 39-40.

based only on quotations or similar phrases from Classical authors, the documentation for the Medieval Latin period is much richer. One would perhaps be justified in assuming that many themes and traditional expressions from the classical period were transmitted through the "learned" literature of Vulgar Latin. It has long been established that Medieval literature, and in fact the Middle Ages in general, were scorned for their obscurity, their confused or incomprehensible thinking. The "anarchical monastic literature" was for a long time a poor cousin in linguistic and literary research. The first bases to serve as a guide for rational studies in this area were provided by the writings of Wilhelm Mayer for literary history and Paul von Winterfeld for history (in the *Monumenta Germaniae Historica*). Salverda de Grave and Frantzen further developed these new and promising areas of research, but Frantzen went too far and postulated these Medieval Latin models as the only possible sources even for the German folk-songs. A systematic investigation was provided by Hennig Brinkmann (*Die Anfänge lateinischer Liebesdichtung im Mittelalter*, 1926), whose research in the area of morphology was very productive. However, his conclusions were to a large extent responsible for the spread of a false generalization. For Brinkmann, the troubadour lyrics represented nothing but secularized religious poetry. A more recent book by P. Dronke analyzes the problem from a broader point of view.

The detailed studies of Scheludko are of first importance. For one thing, he proves that the central notion of *trobar* for "compose poetry" corresponds to the artistic theories of rhetorics, which also saw the creation of poetry as a handicraft. In this sense expressions like *cholorar un chan* (ornament a poem), *polir* (file), *trobar clus, trobar leu* are to be understood as descendants of *ornatus difficilis, ornatus facilis*. The main sources of the rhetorical tradition are to be found in: 1. the two books of Cicero *De inventione*, 2. the four books of Cornificius *Retorica ad Herennium*, 3. Horace's *Epistles to the Pisones*, 4. Alcuin's advice *De rhetorica. Ornatio*, which even in ancient rhetorics was also called *ornatus, elocutio* or λέξις, could be of three kinds, *modus gravis, mediocris, extenuatus* (Faral translates "grave, tempéré, familier" in his authoritative *Les Arts poétiques du XIIe et du XIIIe siècle*). One of the medieval *ars poetica* (the *Documenta* of Geoffroi de Vinsauf) states: "Sunt igitur tres styli, humilis, mediocris, grandiloquus.... Quando enim de generalis personis rebus tractatur, tunc est stylus grandiloquus, quando de humilibus, humilis, quando de mediocribus, mediocris." [6]

Scheludko is not so narrow in scope as to see the religious traditions as the only source. His hypothesis may be summed up as follows: In their conception of love (cf. our chapter IV) the troubadours drew inspiration from religious poetry and, through this in turn, from the pagan and early Christian philosophers in adapted or reworked form. In structure as well, there is undoubtedly a direct influence of secular lyric by religious verse. As for the use of themes, we must look back to rhetorical traditions. For Scheludko, the *art* of the troubadours "came without doubt from the school of medieval Rhetorics." [7] The use of *figurae* as a rhetorical means of expression points unambiguously in that direction. According to rhetorical theory, the *figurae* are divided into *schemata* and *tropi*. By *schemata* are meant plays on words, tendencies toward imitative harmony, syntactic combinations and constructions. *Trobar leu* does not go beyond these rather modest embellishments. The *tropi* are a different matter; these figures are dependent on the meaning of words and are therefore semantic combinations. Among them we find: *synecdoche* (a type of *pars pro toto*; e.g. waves instead of the sea, sail instead of ship); *allegory* (representation of a figurative object in order to call forth the idea of another, a sort of prolonged metaphor; e.g. *Le Roman de la Rose, Pilgrim's Progress*); *metaphor* (originally, according to Aristotle, a synonym for *tropus*; for the rhetoricians, a figure in which the natural meaning of a word is transformed into something different; a sort of abbreviated simile; generally the metaphor is the transference [*metaphora*, to transfer] of semantic content onto a concrete level; e.g. the root of all evil; the well-springs of passion, etc.); *metonymy* (literally "change of name"; this figure attempts to express an object or a notion by means of a term

---

[6] Quoted after Faral, *Les Arts poétiques du XIIe et du XIIIe siècle*, II, 3, 145.

[7] Scheludko, "Beiträge zur Entstehungsgeschichte der altprovenzalischen Lyrik," *Archivum Romanicum*, XV, 1931, p. 139.

which is different in form but connected semantically with it; e.g. cause for effect, active for passive), etc. All of these figures, which demand a greater intellectual effort, were preferred by the poets of *trobar clus*.

The starting point, according to rhetorical theory, is the *inventio materiae*, which corresponds to the *trobar razo*. Thereupon, the poet-craftsman sets about ornamenting his work, that is he proceeds to *amplificatio, circumlocutio ad argumentum et decorum materiae*. Next follows the *contentio*, whose function is to outline the exact opposite of the matter. The *ratiocinatio* often consists of empty phrases and exhausts itself in ergotisms which serve no other purpose than to fill out the work. Among the favourite means, which we find in the Bible and particularly in the Psalms, are *repetitio* and *frequentatio*, that is repetition and sequential grouping of words.

Scheludko believes that the *tornada* may only be explained as a continuation of the literary epistle, which was often joined onto the communication or *messatge*. The art of the epistle may well have played a part in the development, for the five parts required by the *rationes dictandi* are often found in the *canso*, although here the emphasis is on one single section, or on two at the most; other sections may simply be omitted. The five sections are: *salutatio, benevolentiae captatio, narratio, petitio, conclusio*. Out of this Scheludko comes to the conclusion that the classical *canso* of the troubadours is a sort of "epistle of love."[8] The request for love does indeed always contain an introductory part (a celebration of nature, remarks on the theme and occasion of the poem) and generally three sections taken from the epistle structure: 1. *captatio benevolentiae* in praise of the beloved; 2. *expositio* in the explanation and description of the sorrow and pleasures of love; 3. *petitio* in the request for *merce*, favour. The envoi *(tornada)* pays homage to the patron. We know that the troubadours did not alter the contents of the poem, that is its occasion and themes; their art consisted rathed in varying the expression. Because of this, the love lyric became fertile

---

[8] Scheludko, "Religiöse Elemente im weltlichen Liebeslied der Troubadours," *Zeitschrift für französische Sprache und Literatur*, 59, 1935, p. 203.

ground for the most traditional of commonplaces and could develop into manneristic poetry of the best and worst sort. Scheludko's declaration is surely just as valid today: "In this centuries-old literary tradition had been formed a solid amalgam of various elements of style and thought, taken from the dominant literary tradition, in which Christian features played an important role. This combination of different elements of style contributed not only to the refinement of poetic language and form but was also important in the formulation of the conventional concept of love held by the troubadours, which has still not been fully clarified". [9] We shall return to this later.

5. *The Liturgical Theory*

This section wil be intentionally brief, because the chapters on vocabulary and themes will go much more deeply into the question of religious influences during the discussion of specific examples. Lack of space dictates against a presentation here of the interesting hypothesis of Denis de Rougemont, for whom the *canso* gives expression to a Cathar symbol of purity. [10]

"L'art du poète est l'aboutissant d'une lutte qui se livre, chez lui, entre ses sentiments spontanés et les obstacles qui s'opposent à leur expression immédiate." [11] Seldom have these words of de Grave been more fittingly applied to any period of literary history than to that of courtly poetry, which gives form to a tension-laden atmosphere in which the individual stands in fruitful opposition to society, art in opposition to religion. The *canso* is an attempt to gain mastery over this tension. The patterns of thought and daily life of the early medieval people were largely determined by the Church. The liturgical theory, as long as it does not limit itself to formal matters and distorted generalizations (as in Brinkmann), makes no attempt to replace the Medieval Latin theory; rather it

---

[9] *Ibid.*, p. 204.
[10] Cf. Denis de Rougemont, *L'Amour et l'Occident*, Paris², 1954; *Les Mythes de l'amour*, Paris, 1961.
[11] Salverda de Grave, J. J., *Observations sur l'art lyrique de Guiraut de Bornelh*, Amsterdam, 1938, p. 33.

complements the latter by taking full account of the fact that, as Merk says: "the individual lives in the Church and the Church in him." [12] If religion was indeed a living reality, not limited merely to doctrine in daily life, then it must have influenced the poet as well. Scheludko traces the song of repentance back to the hymns and to the Bible, the ballad melodies back to Gregorian chant, and the *alba* back to the liturgical morning-hymn. There is a particularly close connection with the parts of the Mass that were sung. Of great importance for poetry was the Alleluia, which the congregation repeated along with the concluding part or the text which was being sung; from this Errante (cf. *infra*) was able to explain the themes of the Refrain. The canonical hours were also a firmly-anchored and influential institution. There were eight divisions: [13] Matin, Prime, Tierce, Sexte, Nones, Vesper, Completas horas (Old French "complies") and Laud. Prime, Tierce, Sexte and Nones go back, of course, to the Roman divisions of the day. In time the *Laudes matutinae* replaced the *Vigiliae*, that is, the hour of prayer was advanced from two o'clock in the morning to the early daylight hours. Right after Matin early Mass was said. The lack of necessary competence prevents us from going into musical problems, but in general it may be assumed that the influence of religious songs on secular ones was made all the more significant by the fact that the liturgical texts were repeated for the believer every day. A specialist in this area is Spanke.

As early as in the poems of the first troubadour, Guillaume IX, Scheludko perceives the transposition of the Christian concept of love into secular terms. For example, Guillaume required from the lover the same high qualities which are generally connected with *caritas: patientia, humilitas, pietas*. The essential nature of love for the Aquitanian poet-prince is a sort of *summum bonum*. Terms such as "serve" and "beg for mercy and compassion" are strewn throughout his work. It is therefore not surprising to find a mixture of temporal and religious elements from the first

---

[12] Merk, C. J., "Anschauungen über das Leben der Kirche im altfranzösischen Heldenepos," *Zeitschrift für Romanische Philologie, Beiheft*, 41.
[13] Winkler, Maria, *op. cit.*, p. 25.

appearance of secular poetry. Marcabru and his school had only to establish the appropriate accents.

At this point a work, unfortunately of the one-sided variety, must be mentioned, for it drew attention to the liturgical theory. In 1948, there appeared in Florence *Marcabru e le fonti sacre dell'antica lirica romanza* by Guido Errante. Although Marcabru was excluded from our study as being too specifically oriented, the hypotheses of Errante must be briefly outlined because of the dangers that lie hidden in them. The technique of the Refrain, the "pièce de résistance" of the book, represents for Errante the "criterio-base per un ordinamento delle strutture ritmiche dei primi trovatori" (cf. chapter IV). He is entirely correct in rejecting the popular origins of the refrain as a false *communis opinio*. Errante emphasizes as well the close relationship between the lyric and music that accompanies Mass. He says of this: "Anche i più infatigabili esploratori delle zone popolari devono amettere naturalmente l'influsso della chiesa, e non solo sull'elemento emotivo (laude-preghiera), ma anche sugli sviluppi propriamente technici." [14] The quotation may serve also as an example of the polemic tone which mars this scientific work. Errante's attack is directed against Italian scholars active in Europe. The Medieval Latin Refrain structures grew out of the oldest church music, the Psalms, and not out of the hymns which were only introduced into the northern regions toward the end of the fourth century. The role of the people in the *psalmus responsorius* was "interamente passiva." [15] In saying this, Errante is obviously trying to answer the objection made by adherents of the folksong theory, that even in the realm of the Church, the origin of the refrain is to be ascribed to the people. In the ninth-century church, singing was taken over by the *Schola Cantorum,* and only from this period can one clearly see an enrichment of the melodies, perhaps even accompanied by poetic phrasing. The complexity of composition of the texts leads Errante to presume that the idea of a collective creation must be rejected. Scheludko had already revealed (*Archivum Romanicum,* 1931) the discovery of the beginnings of refrain

---

[14] Errante, *Marcabru e le fonti sacre dell'antica lirica romanza*, Florence, 1948, p. 106.
[15] *Ibid.*, p. 106.

patterns in the hymnlike in *matutinis laudibus*. But it is nonetheless undeniably Errante's contribution to have systematically worked out the importance of the responsive chants as direct forerunners of the refrain structure. It should be added that the research of musicologists has conclusively confirmed Errante's theory of the refrain technique. There is no doubt that the liturgical music of the early Middle Ages, and especially the Gregorian chant, was of great importance for the later development of secular poetry. But it is possible that Errante is exaggerating the importance somewhat, since we only possess 264 melodies for Old Provençal songs, as compared with about two thousand for Old French. Is this body of material not too slim to support sweeping conclusions concerning all secular lyrics? It is not impossible that all the melodies that did not conform to orthodox liturgical form were not written down, or were perhaps impossible to transcribe.

The daily familiarity with interesting Biblical passages may have inspired the sensitive believer. The *visitatio sepulchri*, for example, put together from parts of Matthew (28, 1-7) and Luke (1, 46-55), was transformed into musical structure, which gave dramatic tension to the story and greater emphasis to individual sentences, inviting the imaginative believer to creative meditation. Errante is less convincing in the section on sources, particularly when he arranges lines from Marcabru and Biblical quotations in pairs. Contini considers the comparisons that he gives as "vague and unconvincing." [16] Wherever Errante restricts himself to textual exegesis of Marcabru, his work may be regarded as conclusive, but the philosophical part must be used with caution. The lack of bibliographical awareness is quite unpardonable. For example, Salvatore Battaglia's work *I primi trovatori*, Naples, 1940, is simply not mentioned, although some of Errante's conclusions were already drawn by Battaglia. He simply does not mention the possibility of Arabic influence, although Nykl was exploring that problem in America where Errante was working. What Errante has done in fact is to replace the a priori attitudes of the folk-school with a no less definite a priori attitude toward liturgy, which

---

[16] Contini, Gianfranco, Review of Errante, *Belfagor*, IV, 1949, p. 614.

has a few vulnerable spots here and there. In spite of its subjectivity, however, the work is, as Roncaglia says in his review, "uno stimulo efficace" [17] for those who are interested in the troubadours; for specialists on Marcabru the study is indispensable.

---

[17] Roncaglia, Aurelio, Review of Errante, *Cultura Neolatina*, IX, 1949, p. 191.

CHAPTER III

THE TROUBADOURS' CONCEPTION OF LOVE

In erotically-tinged language there is almost always a transcendental tendency, and Maria Winkler is justified in seeing this as the reason why love poetry is drawn involuntarily into the vortex of traditional religious speech patterns without the slightest indication of conscious imitation.[1] This phenomenon is moreover not limited to the area of language alone, for it played just as great a role in the formation of the new conception of love.

Scheludko perceives in the troubadour lyrics a "philosophical attitude toward love,"[2] by which he no doubt means the pronounced tendency toward abstraction in the *canso*. Guillaume IX sings of two things in love: on the one hand, the beloved is an actual person and thus, there is the concomitant reality of the pleasant and unpleasant consequences that are the lot of a lover; on the other hand, love is an abstraction. We know how playful the troubadours' attitude toward abstraction was, speaking to the beloved herself with the words *amor*, *joy* or some adjective used

---

[1] Winkler, *op. cit.*, p. 50. Ignace Feuerlicht carries this sociological point of view even further. He sees in the troubadours' concept of love "a natural flower which sprang directly from the soil of chivalric life and training into the light of art. The service of the Lady, which is inexplicably 'unmanly,' is simply the continuation of a tradition which is indeed unmanly, adolescent; true service of the Lady is only the inner continuation of the hunting code." (Cf. "Vom Ursprung der Minne," *Archivum Romanicum*, 23, 1939, p. 140 ff. The article is reproduced in R. Baehr's anthology *Der provenzalische Minnesang*, Darmstadt, 1967, pp. 263-302).

[2] Scheludko, Dimitri, "Über die Theorien der Liebe bei den Trobadors," *Zeitschrift für Romanische Philologie*, 21, 1940, pp. 204.

as a noun. The abstract in the Middle Ages in general covered a broad semantic field. "A person formed in the medieval type of 'realism' tends to recognize in the common abstract notions an actual existence as an idea or even as a true substantial thing." [3] This fact is one of the freedoms that were first recognized by the Provençal poets in relation to the Latin language, and "the literary artists of Southern France knew how to put this freedom to good use." [4] In the ligth of this, we may speak of both the poetic and the philosophical content of the Provençal love-song.

There are generally three reasons proposed to explain this new attitude which attempts to justify love on metaphysical grounds (cf. chapter V, 10 on mysticism). The influence of Plato is certainly present, but so indirectly that it often cannot be demonstrated in the texts. Likewise the writings of Pesudo-Areopagita (fourth century), translated by Scotus Eriugenus, and of St. Augustine may well have been known to a public interested in philosophy, especially the clerics. Through the latter, a few platonically oriented expressions achieved a certain amount of extension, whether through commentaries or by oral transmission. Ovid was an authoritative model for a few poets who knew his works; in particular, his influence on Barnard de Ventadour is a commonly acknowledged fact. Medieval Christian philosophy must not be overlooked as a third sphere of influence in the formation of the new conception of love. For here, for the first time, theological, philosophical and secular matters were combined with regard to practical ethics. At the same time, Christianity was striving then as now to be universal in the fullest sense of the term and to encompass the area of human love as well. A fourth source which has been ignored for too long, but which played a very real part in twelfth-century life, was the great medieval mysticism, to which a special chapter has been devoted later in this study.

As an example of an ecclesiast who meditated on love, and probably influenced the attitudes of other troubadours besides Marcabru, we may take a passage from Guillaume de St. Thierry's

---

[3] Heinimann, Siegfried, "Das Abstraktum in der französischen Sprache des Mittelalters," *Romanica Helvetica*, 73, 1963, p. 7.

[4] *Ibid.*, p. 55.

(*1085) *De natura et dignitate amoris*. In this work, platonic notions of sublime love are mentioned, taken perhaps from the reading of Areopagita, Scotus and Augustine:

> Ars est artium ars amoris, cujus magisterium sibi retinuit natura et deus auctor naturae. Ipse enim amor a creatore indutus, nisi naturalis ejus ingenuitas adulterinis aliquibus affectibus praepedita fuerit. (Migne 184, 379)
> Spiritus naturali pondere suo, amore suo sursum ferre deberet ad deum qui creavit eum, carnis humiliatus illecebris non intellexit, et comparatus jumentis insipientibus similis factus est illis ....
> Cor ad concupiscentiae carnalis ignem degenere quadam mollitie liquescens totum defluxit in ventrem ... omnie confundens, omnia degenerans, omnia adulterans, amoris naturalem affectum pervertens, in brutum quendam carnis appetitum. (Migne 184, 381)
> Conclusio: A deo solo amor dator. (382) [5]

Scheludko dismisses rather too brusquely the possibilities of comparison with the feudal system, which Wechssler and Köhler in particular (the latter proceeding by sociological methods) see as the point of departure for the concept of love. The fact that *oboedientia* had already been firmly rooted for a long time in the vocabulary of the Church, and had been modelled on the Ovidian *servitium amoris*, is not by any means sufficient justification for ignoring a force which is as much a part of everyday life as the vassal relationship. Courtly poetry is indisputably social poetry, for which reason modern scholars (e.g. Köhler) have had recourse to a new historico-sociological method. "Social changes not only furnish new themes for a seismographically sensitive literature, and change the function of existing ones, they also influence the make-up of the poet himself." [6] Even for those who do not wish to go as far as Köhler, who seems to have considered "the great, very poetic paradox of courtly love, i.e. the renunciation of its fulfillment" as a "sublimated expression of the frustration of the propertyless petty nobility, and therefore stemming from concrete

---

[5] Quoted after Scheludko, "Über die Theorien...," p. 205.
[6] Köhler, Erich: *Trobadorlyrik und höfischer Roman*, Berlin, 1962, p. 6.

socio-economical conditions," [7] still the analogy of the homage paid by the lover to his lady with that of the vassals to their feudal lord is obviously not a forced one. The fact that the feudal system was more systematically developed in the Anglo-Norman and French courts is not a proof of its lack of influence in the south. On the other hand it is considerably easier to demonstrate that sociological considerations did affect the poets, because the code of love and life was consciously constructed on the basis of the most cultivated and refined behaviour possible toward the lady. She is the one who leads the impetuous young men to *mezura*, a sort of applied *sen*; she is the one who first raises the man to the level of true aristocracy by guiding him to *cortezia*. [8] The pursuit of love becomes a publicly conducted concern of a certain social class. "La classe aristocratique avait besoin d'un idéal social et moral nouveau, correspondant au changement survenu dans les moeurs." [9] Even Guillaume, who is often frivolous, demands *oboedientia* (*Pus vezem de novelh florir*, ed. Jeanroy, VII, 25-26, p. 18):

> Ja no sera nuils hom ben fis
> Contr'Amor si non l'es aclis
>
> (Never will any man be well
> suited in matters of love,
> if he does not bow down to it.)

The notion of *oboedientia*, feudalistically conceived and perfected by Christianity, makes love into the source of all virtues and elevates it to the level of a moral principle, through the force of its absolute demands. Thus it is possible that the meaning of love is to be found in the striving of the lover toward perfection. This is doubtless why Köhler sees in the courtly poet "a potential rival of the theologians." [10]

Still another dualistic point of view contributed to the refinement of the conception of love—one that vacillates back and forth between success and renouncement, between the normal

---

[7] *Ibid.*, p. 6.
[8] Cf. for example, Raimbaut's enumeration of the specifically courtly virtues, P. C. 238, 2.
[9] Lazar, *op. cit.*, p. 10.
[10] Köhler, *op. cit.*, p. 17.

active life and asceticism. The forced or chosen spiritualization of erotic drives must also be assessed as a serious attempt to bring about their social capacities. Myrrha Lot-Borodine undoubtedly views content somewhat too idealistically when she interprets the troubadours' conception of love as "le don de soi désintéressé, la gratuité du service ou *l'amour qui est sa propre fin*." [11] Aside from the fact that erotic intent is often openly stated in the *canso*, the ethically-conceived notion of "amour-vertu" is not as selfless as it might seem to be, for the elevation of the lady to the divine level, her apotheosis, also has in view, as part of the intellectual fiction, the elevation of the man to the level of a hero of virtue. Lot-Borodine rejects the generalizing interpretations of courtly love as the glorification of an adulterous passion. [12] Scheludko had already pointed out that the poet sings of his love for the lady in the poem proper, whereas in the *tornada* he generally praises only the patron or patroness to whom the poem is addressed. Whenever the lover is speaking of his protectors he keeps careful check on what he says, but concerning *midons* he expresses himself freely.

There have been several attempts to distinguish arbitrarily two "opposed" poetical schools: [13] the Idealists and the Realists. According to Jeanroy, Jaufré Rudel and Bernard de Ventadour represent the Idealists and are "des poètes courtois." [14] Their style, he says, is selective and noble and has a transcendental function toward a newly created conception of love: the *Fin' Amors*. The Realists, on the other hand, are fervent defenders of the traditional conception of love. They attack the *Fin' Amors* vigourously in the name of Christian ethics. Marcabru and, to some extent, Cercamon would represent this tendency. But, as always, classifications of this kind are limited to a few examples, for many Provençal poets do not belong exclusively to either one of these categories but rather oscillate from one to the other,

---

[11] Lot-Borodine Myrrha, "Sur les origines et les fins du 'service d'amour' provençal," *Mélanges Jeanroy*, Paris, 1928, p. 225; reproduced in *De l'amour profane à l'amour sacré*, Paris, 1961, pp. 71-88.
[12] *Ibid.*, p. 225.
[13] Cf. the approach of Appel, Hoepffner, Jeanroy and Riquer.
[14] *La Poésie lyrique des troubadours*, Paris, 1934, vol. I, p. 13.

sometimes even in a single poem. Guillaume IX and Marti illustrate this ambivalence. [15]

Lazar, a partisan of the profane love conception, maintains that the troubadours' protest against carnal possession is merely made in order to lead astray potential critics. [16] With the same justification, based primarily upon the concept of a "game for the sake of a game" (which is not too far from "art for art's sake") as found in the *Partimen*, it is not impossible to imagine that many troubadours did not need a real response from the beloved. Rather they developed the absence of an answer to a dramatic theme which is psychologically and intellectually much more interesting than the common love story. Father Denomy, in his detailed study on *Fin' Amors*, concludes that "it is a love wherein desire is not the end in itself but a means to the end, progress and growth in virtue, merit and worth. It is the latter which is at the base of Courtly Love and not desire. Desire is an integral part, an essential part but what is of the very essence of Courtly Love is its ennobling power, the elevation of the lover effected by a ceaseless desire and yearning for the love of the worthy lady." [17] Even if one does not concur with this moral point of view one cannot deny the virtually unlimited spectrum of interpretation which many ambiguous troubadour poems allow. For Lazar, the *Fin'Amors* "est une casuistique de la passion amoureuse [...] [et] par son essence même, un amour adultère." [18] He is, it seems to me, successful in showing that the *Fin'Amors* is not a purely contemplative love. Often the troubadour expects everything from the lady, *del surplus*. However, it is difficult if not impossible to determine whether he is playing an artistic game rooted in a very sophisticated casuistic of love or whether he truly desires a real woman. Clearly,

---

[15] For an excellent "mise au point" see Lazar, *op. cit.*, particularly chapter II: "Idéologie et casuistique de la *Fin'Amors*," p. 47 sq.

[16] See *op. cit.*, p. 73 sq.

[17] Denomy, "Fin'Amors: The Pure Love of the Troubadours, Its Amorality and Possible Source," *Mediaeval Studies*, VI, 1945, p. 175. "Jaufré Rudel's *amour lointain* is an expression of *fin'amors, bon'amors*. Its object is a fair lady (II, 17-19; V, 31-32). It matters little whether she be real, fictitious, the fancied embodiment of the perfection of womanhood, she is unattainable; his is a love of desire not of possession." (*Ibid.*, p. 164).

[18] *Op. cit.*, pp. 54-55; 63.

the nature of his imagined or real feelings is *profane* and not spiritual. In either case the poet is dealing with a reality, be it a physical one or the reality of a dream.

To sum up, one may say that the *obedientia, reverentia, servitus, obsequium, servitium, subjectio, humilitas,* etc., demanded by the lady probably stem directly form religious vocabulary, but that it had already belonged for a long time to the language of rhetoric as well, for example, the epistolary style of the salutation.[19] The practical application of the notion of *oboedientia* in feudal terminology leads almost necessarily to the analogy between the service of love and the service of the vassal.

The contrition and persistent despair that is part of so many of the poems arises perhaps from the fact that the image of the lady which the troubadour creates for himself does not correspond to reality. In time he discovers a sort of pleasure in this incongruous state of affairs, which in any case becomes his most important source of inspiration. He may sing of his unfulfilled desires and the emotions they call forth. The *topos* of frustrated desire reaches its fullest expression in the songs of Peire Vidal, who sometimes goes as far as the glorification of disillusionment. The "volupté chrétienne de la résignation"[20] is at stake here; yet this is only a small fragment in the complicated mosaic of the troubadours' conception of love, which Lot-Borodine aptly calls "une métaphysique de l'amour profane."[21]

---

[19] Cf. Krüger, P., *Bedeutung und Entwicklung der "salutatio,"* Greifswald, 1912, pp. 24 sq.
[20] Lot-Borodine, *op. cit.,* p. 227.
[21] *Ibid.,* p. 229.

Chapter IV

THE VOCABULARY OF *CORTEZIA*

The present chapter on vocabulary offers a selection of nouns and verbs whose formation was influenced to a greater or lesser degree by the language of the Church. Care is taken to differentiate between typically religious words and mixed religious and secular terms. In the troubadours' language we find:

A) Nouns of a typically religious nature: *sagramen, sacrificamen, baptisteri, ostia, confesamen, confesion, comunication, benezion, asolt, sepulcre, sermon, oferenda, meravelha, devocion, caritat, pelegrinatge, gracia, pietat, fes*, etc., all of which are terms belonging to the technical vocabulary of theology and are therefore outside the field of interest of the present study.

Of significance, however, in the secular lyric are: *penedensaria, pecat, colpa, merces, almorna, mana, obediensa, martir*.

B) Nouns of mixed nature: *midons, pasio, joy, solatz, deport, deduch*.

C) Religious verbs (many of them which are related to the nouns mentioned above are omitted from consideration): *pregar, adorar, orar, batejar*.

D) Verbs of mixed nature: *falhir, servir, guerir*.

A) 1. *penedensaria* and *penedense* < "poenitentia" plus the normal suffix of abstraction *-aria*. The Classical Latin sense of "repentance" was broadened by Church Latin. Whoever repents of something is a penitent, and from this came the meaning of "atonement, punishment." Bernard de Ventadour uses *penedensa* in an entirely secular poem *Lo tems vai e ven e vire* (ed. Lazar, *B. de Ventadour, Chansons d'amour*, Paris, 1966, 44, 31-32, p. 232) in which he is complaining of the harshness of the beloved:

> Qui vid anc mais penedensa
> Faire denan lo pechat?

> (Who ever saw punishment given before the sin?)

Aimeri de Belmont, *Ja n'er credutz* (quoted by Raynouard, *Lexique Roman*, IV, p. 489):

> Anc nuls amantz ni nuls penedensiers
> N'an trais lo mal ni la dolor ni l'ars
> Qu'eu ai sufert plus de cinq ans entiers.

> (No lover, no penitent have experienced the pain or the grief or the ardor I have suffered more than five full years.)

2. *pecat* < *peccatum*. *Peccare* originally meant "to stumble" (e.g. in Horace), then "to make a mistake." The meaning "to sin" in the specifically Christian sense first apeared in the writings of the Fathers of the Church. The *nomen agentis* was not even formed until the time of Church Latin *(peccator)*. Very early the word was used in the Romance Language areas in the meaning "mistake, misdemeanour, fault, etc." The common expression *pecat criminal* (deadly sin) is responsible for the fact that the religious connotation of the word was always present. Thus: Bernard de Ventadour, *Lo gens tems de pascor* (ed. Lazar, 17, 47-48, p. 126):

> E si d'aisso·m vol mal,
> Pechat fai criminal.

> (If she wants to hurt me on that account she is committing a deadly sin.)

Arnaud de Mareuil, *Domna, genser que no sai dir* (ed. Berry, *Florilèges des Troubadours*, Paris, 1930, p. 230):

> Totz vius per vos art e aflam,
> Mas per merce·us, domna, reclam
> Que·m perdones, s'eu falh ni pec.

(I burn alive and I decay for you. But for mercy's sake, lady, I want you to forgive me it I have failed or sinned.)

Peire Vidal, *Plus que·l paubres que jatz el ric ostal* (ed. Anglade, *Les poésies de Peire Vidal*, Paris, 1913, XVIII, 17, p. 57):

> Si m'ajust Deus, peccat fai criminal
> Ma bela domna, car ilh no·m soccor:

(By God, she commits a criminal sin, my fair lady, for she does not succour me.)

Peire d'Auvergne (ed. Rudolf Zenker, *Die Lieder des Peires von Auvergne*, Erlangen, 1900, p. 122):

> Qu'el segl'ai fag mon plazer
> Tan qu'en sui de trop peccaire.

(For in the world I have had my pleasure to such an extent that I am thereby too much a sinner.)

3. *colpa* < *culpa*, a commonplace, thanks no doubt, to the *mea culpa* of Mass. The Provençal *faire sa colpa* meant "to say one's triple 'mea culpa'." This decidedly religious word must have been on the way toward archaism, that is, in time it must have called forth the same effect as Modern French *coulpe*. For "fault, mistake" there were other terms available: *falta, fauta, pecat, mesfach, forfach, forfatura*. If *colpa* was nevertheless used, then it was in order to suggest a particular meaning by means of the religious association. The *mea culpa* is faintly echoed in Bernard de Ventadour, *Conortz era sai eu be* (ed. Lazar, 15, 17 and 29-30, p. 116):

> Per ma colpa m'esdeve

(It happens to me through my guilt.)

Ibid.,

> E s'eu en amar mespren,
> Tort a qui colpa m'en fai,

(And should I be wrong in loving, it would be error to think I am guilty,) and in Giraut de Bornelh, *Totz tems me sol* (ed. Kolsen, 2 vol., Halle, 1910/1935, V, 63):

> Ni no deu sa colpa celar
>
> (He must not conceal his own guilt.)

4. *merces* < *merces, -edis*, accusative *mercem* in Vulgar Latin; cf. Ernout Meillet, *Dictionaire Etymologique de la langue Latine;* [1] "wages, price of an article," figuratively "reward, punishment." The troubadours used it in this sense but also in the sense of *mercem Dei*, "the grace of God," which developed in Medieval Latin, principally in Church Latin. In addition, they very often used the word in the related sense of "compassion, charity" (Classical Latin *misericordia*). The Provençal poets have a special liking for the expression *clamar merce*, "beg for mercy," which naturally comes from the realm of theology. Instead of begging for mercy, the lady is entreated. The notion of mercy developed into a topos (cf. Themes). *Merces* can also mean "forgiveness," as in Guillaume IX, *Pos de chantar m'es pres talentz* (ed. Jeanroy, *Les Chansons de Guillaume IX*, Paris², 1964, XI, 21-24, p. 27-28):

> Merce quier a mon compaignon,
> S'anc li fi tort qu'il m'o perdon;
> Et ieu prec en Jesu del tron
> Et en romans et en lati.
>
> (I beg forgiveness of my companion. Should I have harmed him, may he forgive me. And [thus] I pray Jesus, King of Heaven, in Roman as well as in Latin.)

Or in Alfred de Sestaro, *En mon cor*, II:

> E si·m fai mal, a, merces s·en aveigna!
>
> (And if she treats me badly [love or the lady, both interpretations are possible] ah, then may she be forgiven for it!)

---

[1] Cf. also Lerch, Eugen, "Trobadorsprache und religiöse Sprache," *Cultura Neolatina*, III, 1943, p. 215, where *merces* is mentioned as a notion from the religious tradition.

The word *merces* is used so often in the *canso* that all the occurrences can scarcely be counted (cf. Themes).

5. *almorna* < Vulgar Latin *alemosina*, Church Latin *eleemosyna*, originally Greek ἐλεμοσύνη, which meant "pity," but used as early as the New Testament in the sense of "alms." Bernard de Ventadour uses it in the older sense with relation to the pitiless lady *Non es meravelha s'eu chan* (ed. Lazar, 1, 47-48, p. 62):

> E d'ome qu'es assi conques
> Pot domn'aver almorna gran:
>
> (And for such a clearly defeated man the lady could show great pity.)

6. *mana, manna* < *manna*, a Hebraism meaning the celestial bread of the Israelites. This Biblical word was used metaphorically in addition to its specifically religious meaning, as in Jaufré Rudel, *Quan lo rius de la fontana* (ed. Jeanroy, *Les Chansons de Jaufré Rudel,* Paris, 1924, II, 20-21, p. 4):

> Ben es selh pagutz de mana
> Qui ren de s'amor guazanha!
>
> (He who knows how to draw profit from his love is truly provided with celestial bread.)

7. *obediensa* < *oboedientia, oboedire*, "allegiance, obedience." *Oboedire* was formed on the root of *audire*, so that it meant literally "to listen to someone," then by extension "to obey." *Oboedire* often appears along with *obtemperare*, as, for example, in the Vulgate. The *FEW* has this to say concerning the matter: "It was [...] borrowed through the French and applied principally in the sphere of religious and legal use." It was easy for the word to be accepted into the vocabulary of feudalism because of its use in legal matters. Scheludko is wrong to reject out of hand the obvious analogy of lady/lover and feudal lord/vassal, because it is supported by the common notion of obedience. In Old French too, according to the *FEW* in the *Psautier d'Oxford,* the learned use of the word in the Church and in law stood in the way of popular development, in which the "b" would have fallen out. *Obéir* in Old French means "se soumettre

aux ordres de quelqu'un et les exécuter"; that is precisely what the troubadours were accustomed to doing in relation to their ladies, and the vassals in relation to their feudal lords. Guillaume IX, *Pos de chantar m'es pretz talentz* (ed. Jeanroy, XI, 2-3, p. 26):

> Farai un vers, don sui dolenz:
> Mais non serai obedienz
>
> (I will compose a verse which grieves me: I will never be a servant of love anymore.)

Peire Vidal, *Ges pel temps per e brau* (ed. Anglade, XXIII, 22-23, p. 72):

> Sui vostres bendizens
> E sers obediens,
>
> (I am the singer of your praise and your obedient servant.)

8. *martir* < Medieval Latin *martyrium*, "martyrdom," originally a Church Latin word meaning "a sacrificial death for one's belief," soon used as well in the extended senses of "bloodbath, slaughter, plague, need, torment, affliction, agony, etc." The original meaning, particularly the element of self-sacrifice for a higher ideal, can often be felt in the troubadours. The word may be considered a part of the affective vocabulary. It is synonymous with *tormen*.

Example: G. Pierre de Casals, *Ja taut* (quoted in Raynouard, *Lexique Roman*, IV, p. 162):

> De martir poga far confes
> Mi dons ab un bays solamens
>
> (My lady could only confess the martyrdom with a kiss.)

Giraut Riquier, *Ab plazen* (ed. Raynouard, *Choix*, I, 17, p. 461):

> E'l ser, dobla m·mon martir,
> (In the evening my suffering is doubled.)

Arnaut de Mareuil, *Domna, genser que no sai dir* (ed. Berry *Florilèges*, p. 230):

> Domna, no us puesc lo cente dir
> De las penas, ni del martir.

(Lady, I cannot describe to you the hundreth part of the suffering and sacrifice.) Here we have the secular term *pena* for suffering.

Peire Cardenal, *Tot atressi* (quoted by Raynouard, p. 162):

> El cavalgar e'l dormir
> E'l juec d'amor tenon de gran martire.

(Riding horses, sleeping and the game of love are linked to great suffering.)

B) 1. *mi dons; mi* is an old vocative form; the normal form in Old Provençal is *meus, mieus,* or *mia.* Schultz-Gora says: "In *mi dons* the Latin vocative from 'mi' seems to have been preserved." [2] *Mi domina* would have given *mi domna,* therefore *mi dons* cannot have developed from that form.

Regarding the semantic development Lerch suggests: "Are we to take this as nothing more than a facetious exchange of gender, as shown by the use of 'mon chéri,' for example, in addressing a beloved one? May not *mi dons* rather be 'mi domine' (my Lord God)?" [3] Even the Mother of Christ was addressed as: "De mi dons sancta Maria" (*Vie de Sainte Enimie,* fol. 38), "of my lady, blessed Mary."

This is clearly an example of the secularized religion of love (cf. the chapter on themes). According to the *FEW, don* is of secondary formation "taken over by the troubadours along with other feudal expressions to designate the lady served by the poet, especially in conjunction with the personal pronoun."

Mi dons is in any case of religious origin, even more obviously since it is often used as a synonym for *sanctus* (cf. *FEW* on this point). On the other hand, it must be noted that *dominus* as a

---

[2] Schultz-Gora, *Altprovenzalisches Elementarbuch,* par. 118.
[3] Lerch, E., *op. cit.,* p. 215.

Christian word was very soon sharply rivalled by *senior,* so that it could be considered as a secular term by the time of the troubadours, except in a specifically liturgical context. Examples are not necessary.

2. *Pasio, passio, pasiu* < *passio,* an abstract verbal noun derived from *pati,* meaning "suffering, endurance," later especially "the suffering of Christ," figuratively also "sickness, pain."

The Fathers of the Church, Ambrosius and Augustine, were the first to apply *passio* to emotion *(motus animi),* as the Stoics had done earlier with πάδος. Alongside the passive, morally indifferent components deriving from Aristotle, there developed an active *passio* which manifested itself in the eighteenth-century "sentiments" (cf. Themes).

3. *joy, joi* < *gaudium* poses complex problems, a complete discussion of which would exceed the limits of this study. Only the essential matters will be touched upon.

a. *The Etymology*

Gaudium, found almost exclusively in the plural in Classical Latin, gave two forms in Old Provençal: *gaug* and *joy.* FEW says: "Whereas in most of the Romance languages the living forms go back to the singular, Gallo-Roman is divided: south of the Loire-Vosges line are found forms developed from the singular, while to the north are found forms which came from the Latin plural." In the north, then, *gaudia* developed to *joie.* This abstract noun penetrated into the south as well and resulted in *joia* which, however, is much less frequent than *joy.* Nevertheless, its occasional use was sufficient to play a part in the formation of Italian *joia.* Old Provençal *joia* could also have the meaning of "jewel."

The regularly-developed form *gaug* was rivalled by a Poitevin dialectal form *joy* which apparently became widely used through the influence of Guillaume IX. Both forms *joy* and *gaug* existed side by side, but with a semantic differentiation. Lerch considers *joy* to be a contamination of Old French *joie,* and the native word *gaug.*

b. *The Semantics*

Gaudium is of course not the only Latin word for "pleasure"; *laetitia* was also used. "Latin 'gaudium' was used principally to express the feeling, while 'laetitia' had to do more with its manifestation." *(FEW) Laetitia* became *leesse* in Old French, *liesse* in Modern French. The Old Provençal *let* comes from *laetum*. *Laetitia* itself did not serve to denote happiness in Old Provençal. Instead there was a semantic differentiation between the two forms *gaug* and *joy* tending toward the same division of meaning. *Joy* in particular became a key word in the *canso*, embracing an extremely broad semantic field but in time losing much of its forcefulness through overuse. It is generally found in the sense of "pleasure, joy" and, strangely enough, rarely appears in rhyme. *Joy* is a perfect example of the type of word used both in the secular and religious spheres. Here again the double meaning of the word was undoubtedly the reason for its popularity. *Gaug*, on the other hand, is used in contexts where the sensual element predominates. There are of course exceptions, that is, some of the secondary troubadours treat *joy* and *gaug* as synonyms. *Joy d'amor* is used as an almost automatic formula, but *gaug d'amor* is never found.

Gaudium in the sense of religious joy is found in the Vulgate. In Luke 2, 10 the birth of the Saviour is proclaimed: "Nolite timere, ecce enim evangelio vobis gaudium magnum." *Gaudium* and *laetitia* appear early too as a paired expression, as in the troubadours *joy/deport, joy/solatz,* e.g. Isaiah 35, 10: "Et redempti a Domino convertentur ... gaudium et laetitiam obtinebunt." In Augustine we even find a hymn to spiritual joy "O gaudium super gaudium, vincens omne gaudium, extra quod non est gaudium. ... Ibi gaudium infinitum," (quoted by Lerch). Similar is the same joy which is glorified in song after a misadventure by Jaufré Rudel, the poet of *amor de lonh;* maybe it is a "joie spirituelle," as says Jeanroy,[4] unsullied by any *concupiscentia; Belhs m'es l'estius e.l temps floritz* (ed. Jeanroy, IV, 8-9, p. 9):

---

[4] Jeanroy, Alfred, *Les Chansons de Jaufré Rudel,* Paris, 1924, p. V. Jeanroy's conclusions, however, have to be read with caution.

> Er ai ieu e suy jauzitz
> E restauratz en ma valor,

(Now I have joy and am happy and restored to my worth.) Jaufré is even more clearly religious in the same poem (24-25): [5]

> Quar a mon joy suy revertitz:
> E laus en lieys e Dieu e lor

(For I have returned to my [pure] joy and I praise her, God and them [advisors] for it.)

Jeanroy comments in his introduction: "Avec Dieu il remercie certains 'bons conseillers' et une dame (lieys) dans laquelle je reconnais volontiers, comme M. Appel, la Vierge Marie." [6]

Joy and *joven* (youth) form another very commonly paired expression, used to describe the indispensable attributes of true *amor*. Guillaume IX leads the way once more, *Companho, faray un vers ... covinen* (ed. Jeanroy, I, 3, p. 1):

> Et er totz mesclatz d'amor e de joy e de joven.
>
> (And it [the poem] will be made up of love, joy, and youthfulness.)

Around *joy* are grouped a few other words related in meaning which also come from the religious background: *solatz, deport, deduch.*

4. *solatz* < Vulgar Latin *solacium*, Classical *solatium*, "solace," which is preserved in Modern French *soulager*. Semantically the word is closely related to *joy*. Already in Church Latin *solacium* could mean "delight, relief, relaxation, cheering up," close to the Modern French *sérénité*. In the troubadours there was a clear-cut semantic change from *solace* to *joy*. Lerch sees once more the Vulgate as responsible for the change which is already to be found there [7] in Second Corinthians 7. 4: "repletus sum consolatione, superabundo gaudio..." Even the paired expression *joy/*

---

[5] Not I, 22 as Lerch erroneously indicates.
[6] Jeanroy, A., *op. cit.*, p. V.
[7] Cf. Lerch, *op. cit.*, p. 217.

solatz may be seen in the Vulgate in the linking of *consolatione/gaudio*. When the troubadours took over this pair of words, a partial leveling occurred, with the result that *joy* and *solatz*, in spite of their origins, must have often been thought of as synonymous in the sense of *joy*.

There are also passages in which *solatz* clearly means *solace*, as in Marcabru's famous pastoral, *A la fontana del vergier* (ed. Berry, *Florilèges*, VI, 7, p. 196):

> Selha que non vol mon solatz
> (She who does not desire my solace.)

5. *De(s)port*, derived from *(de)portare*, with the meaning "pleasure, joy," related to the modern word "sport" (cf. English "disport"). Lerch reads the meaning of "consolation" into the word as well but finds only one debatable example for it. The primary meaning of *deport* then is still "pleasure, amusement." Example: Guillaume IX, *Pos de chantar m'es pres talentz* (ed. Jeanroy, XI, 39-40, p. 29):

> Qu'eu ai avut joi e deport
> Loing e pres e a mon aizi
>
> For I have found joy and entertainment [Jeanroy translates 'joie et liesse'] far and near and in my home.)

On the basis of Old French *soi deporter*, "to console oneself," Lerch believes that in the following passage *deport* may mean "consolation": Guillaume IX, *Farai un vers de dreyt nien* (ed. Jeanroy, IV, 33, p. 8):

> Quan non la vey, be m'en deport

The translation "I console myself for it, I refuse to be affected by it" is indeed possible here, but so is "I take pleasure in it, I don't care about it," which would reflect more closely the cynical character of the poem and the poet. Besides, this is a verbal use and not conclusive with regard to the noun.

6. *De(s)duch* was "formed from *duire* under the influence of Latin 'deducere'" *(FEW)*; Modern French *déduit*, "amusement,

pastime"; the hunting term *déduit de chasse*, meaning everything belonging to the hunt, is archaic. *Deduch* appears less frequently than *solatz, deport* or *joy*. Originally it meant "tearing oneself away from something unpleasant," then "taking delight in something," which is also the sense of the Old French *se desduire*.

The process of semantic levelling which affected the series *joi, solatz, deport, deduch* is visible already in the Vulgate. Quite often the words *gaudium, laetitia, exultatio* and *consolatio* may be found used in pairs or groups and not always clearly distinguished semantically.

C) 1. *pregar, preyar* < *precari*, "to pray, ask, beg," the mingling of secular and religious connotations already being characteristic of Classical Latin.

Religious meaning: Aimeric de Belenoi, *Ailas! per que viu logamen ni dura* (ed. Dumitrescu, *Poésies du troubadour Aimeric de Belenoi*, Paris, 1935, XII, 45, p. 117):

> Senher, Dieu prec la vostr'arma ampar,
>
> (My lord, I pray God to receive your soul.)

Secular meaning: Gaucelm Faidit, *No m'alegra* (quoted in *Lexique Roman*, IV, p. 621):

> L'irai pregar a sos pes
>
> (I will go to entreat her at her feet.)

Also in the *Vida* of Peire Vidal (ed. Lommatzsch, *Provenz. Liederbuch*, p. 119):

> E totas las [domnas] pregava d'amor.

Bernard de Ventadour, *Amics Bernartz de Ventadorn* (ed. Lazar, 28, 22-28, p. 168):

> Peire, si fos dos ans o tres
> Lo segles faihz al meu plazer,
> De domnas vos dic eu lo ver:
> Non foran mais preyadas ges,
> Ans sostengran tan greu pena

> Qu'elas nos feiran tan d'onor
> C'ans nos prejaran que nos lor.

(Peter, if for two or three years I could determine the course of the world, I tell you the women would not be implored anymore, indeed, they would rather suffer such grief that they would do us the honor to implore us rather than the opposite.)

Id., Lo tems vai e ven e vire (ed. Lazar, 44, 33, p. 234):

> On plus la prec, plus m'e dura;

(The more I supplicate her, the more she is cruel to me.)

Aimeric de Belenoi, *S'a midons planha* (ed. Dumitrescu, XI, 83, p. 111):

> Ylh lau mon chan, e prec li fort que·l playa.

(May she praise my song and may it please her, I beg her strongly.)

2. *adorar* < *adorare*, also with a double connotation in Classical Latin: "worship, pray, entreat" in relation to the gods, the ancestors, and later the Christian God.

Religious meaning: *Histoire abrégée de la Bible* (quoted by Raynouard, *Lexique Roman,* I, p. 28):

> Aysi com servidor et adorador de Dieu

(As a servant and worshipper of God.)

Secular meaning: Gaucelm Faidit, *D'un dolz bel* (quoted by Raynouard, *Lexique Roman,* I, p. 28):

> Car lieis am e lieis ador

(For I love and worship her.)

Of course the Virgin Mary was also worshipped rather than petitioned. But the influence of the cult of the Virgin on the poetry of the troubadours was secondary (cf. Themes).

3. *orar* < *orare* lies within the same field of meaning, but is much less frequent. It can also mean "to wish." *Orare* is the officially accepted Church Latin term for praying. The imperative is found in many of the liturgical prayers which were spoken aloud by the priest: *oremus;* but also in the prayer to the Virgin Mary: *ora pro nobis.* We find an interesting secular use of *orare* in Old Provençal in Folquet de Romans, *Donna ieu pren* (quoted by Raynouard, *Lexique Roman*, p. 37):

> Ieu vos or entre mos bratz
> Que non i sai far autr'orazon.

> (I pray to you in my arms, since I cannot formulate any other prayer [of love; 'orazon' also belongs in this category].)

Jaufré Rudel, *Quan lo rossinhols el folhos* (ed. Jeanroy, I, 9-10, p. 1):

> Quar no sai joya plus valen,
> C'or e desir,

> (For I do not know of any more worthy joy I beg and desire.)

4. *batejar* < *baptizare*, a technical Church Latin term used in Old Provençal, as in Modern French *baptiser*, in the sense of "call, name":
Raimbaut d'Orange, *Escotatz mas no sai que·s es* (ed. Appel, *Provenzalische Chrestomathie*, Leipzig², 1902, XXXVI, 47-48, p. 77):

> Er fenisc mon no·sai-que·s-es
> Qu'aissi l'ai volgut bateiar

> (Now I have finished my whatever-it-is, for that is what I have chosen to call it.)

D) 1. *falhir* < Vulgar Latin *fallire*, Classical *fallere, falli,* "to cause to slide" (Liv. "glacies fallit pedes"), "deceive" (Cic. "Id me non fefellit"): the passive infinitive already meant "to deceive oneself" in Classical Latin. Likewise we find *fallere* meaning "to fail in one's duty" in Classical Latin (Cic. "fallere fidem datam," "to fail to live up to one's word"); semantically related to the religious term *peccare* (cf. *pecat*, above).

The meaning "to fail in one's duty" is still preserved in Catalan. *FEW* says: "In Modern French 'faillir' is gradually losing various of its meanings once again to 'manquer'." In general it may be said that Old French *faillir* and Old Provençal *falhir* have the meaning of "ne pas rendre un service qu'on était en droit d'attendre d'une persone ou d'une chose, laisser quelqu'un dans l'embarras" *(FEW)*. *Falhir* is, strictly speaking, "to sin by omission," then, more generally, "to sin." Lerch's comment on the vocabulary of Guillaume IX is valid for all the words mentioned in this chapter. They compose "such ambiguous expressions, vacillating between the religious and the secular."[8] Example: Guillaume IX, *Mout jauzens me prenc en amar* (ed. Jeanroy, IX, 45-46, p. 24):

> [...] tan tem falhir
> No l'aus m'amor fort assemblar;

> I do not dare to express my love clearly to her, so fearful am I of making a false step.)

Bernard de Ventadour, *Bel m'es qu'eu chan en aquel mes* (ed. Lazar, 41, 38-39, p. 222):

> E s'eu ai falhit ni mespres
> Per trop amar ni per temer,
> Doncs que farai?

> (And if I have slipped and gone astray by loving or fearing too much, what shall I then do?)

Id., Lonc tems a qu'eu no chantei mai (ed. Lazar, 19, 50-51, p. 134):

> Vol me doncs midons aucire,
> Car l'am? O que lh'ai falhit?

> (Does my lady then wish to kill me because I love her? In what way have I failed her?)

---

[8] Cf. Lerch, *op. cit.*, p. 215.

Id., Ab joi mou lo vers e·l comens (ed. Lazar, 3, 15, p. 68):

> C'ades tem om vas so c'ama, falhir,
>
> (For a man is always fearful of sinning against the one he loves.)

2. *servir* < *servire*, "to serve," originally as a slave. *Servir* was used in both the religious and the secular sense and was particularly influenced by feudalism. [9]

Example: Aimeric de Pegulhan, *Ara parra qual seran enveyos* (ed. Appel, LXXIII, 21-22, p. 110):

> Non devria esser hom temeros
> De suffrir mort el servizi de Dieu,
>
> (Man should not be afraid to suffer death in the service of God.)

In spite of the tendency for the word to be secularized because of the influence of feudalism, the religious element remained strongly present, since the principle of the crusades was thought of as *service de Dieu*. The dedication of the vassal, which could go as far as death, was incorporated into the troubadours' conception of love because of its absolute nature.

Example: Bernard de Ventadour, *Non es meravelha s'eu chan* (ed. Lazar, I, 49-51, p. 62):

> Bona domna, re no·us deman
> Mas que·m prendatz per servidor,
> Qu'e·us servirai com bo senhor,
>
> (Good lady, I ask nothing of you but that you accept me as a servant, for I will serve you like a good master.)

Peire Vidal, *Anc no mori per amor ni per al* (ed. Anglade, XXIV, 9-16, p. 76):

---

[9] For a point of view which emphasizes the courtly structure of the troubadours' love conception rooted in its reverential character, cf. Leo Pollmann, *Die Liebe in der hochmittelalterlichen Literatur Frankreichs, Versuch einer historischen Phänomenologie*, Frankfurt, 1966, particularly part II: "Die Rehabilitierung der profanen Liebe im Bereich der Trobadors," pp. 73-193. He points out that "the troubadours bends [...] before the social incarnation of courtly power and civility" which his *midons* represents.

Bona domna, vostr'ome natural
Podetz, si·us platz, leugieramant aucir:
Mas a la gen vo·n faretz escarnir
E pois auretz en peccat criminal.
Vostr'om sui be, que ges no·m tenh per meu,
Mas be laiss' om a mal senhor son feu;
E pois val pauc rics hom, quan pert sa gen,
Qu'a Daire.l re Persa fo parven.

(Good lady, if you wish you may easily kill your liege: but people will blame you for it and you will have committed a mortal sin. I surely am your man, for I do not possess myself; but you abandon your fief to a bad master; and a powerful man losing his vassal is not worth much, as Darius, King of Persia, had to experience.)

3. *guerir* < Germanic *warjan*, originally meaning "to defend, protect," then figuratively from the twelfth century "to grow well, recover." *(FEW)* The forms *garir, guarir* are also found in Old Provençal. This word is another which belongs to the group of ambiguous terms vacillating between religious and secular connotation. Thus *guerir* can have the sense of "recover from the malady of love" (there are innumerable examples, some of them metaphorical in nature), but it is also occasionally used to mean *salvare*, "heal, save, redeem"

Example: Jaufré Rudel, *Quan lo rossinhols el folhos* (ed. Jeanroy, I, 38-39, p. 3):

No sai com ja mais sia pros
Ni cum ja venh'a guerimen

(I do not know he can ever be gallant or ever achieve salvation.)

Gaucelm Faidit, *Per joi del* (quoted in Raynouard, III, 431):

Ai fag la penedensa
E suy del peccat querrits.

(I have done penance and have been freed from sin.)

Aimeric de Belenoi, *No·m laissa ni·m vol retener* (ed. Dumitrescu, V, 20 and 31-32, p. 81):

Quar lieys que·m pot guerir no·m planh

(For she who can save me does not pity me.)

D'aquest mal no·m pot pro tener
Res, mas silh que no·m vol guerir;

(Against this illness there is no medicine except the one that does not want to cure me.)

The trends towards a secularization are already visible in the use of quite a diverse religious vocabulary by some of the Old Provençal poets. This secularization, however, was a rather complexe process. On one hand, there is, no doubt, the constant exposure of these poets as well as of their readers and listeners to a vocabulary already solidly established in a religious context; i.e. in the mass and the activities of the Church in general. On the other hand, the parallel between spiritual love and secular love is as old as mankind. We are, therefore, hardly surprised that, depending on which of both types of love is prevalent, a creative writer sometimes borrows, sometimes even copies the patterns of thinking and speaking of its counterpart. We have also to keep in mind that, after all, the separation between spiritual and carnal love is an artificial one, upheld and emphasized by the concerned type of lover, in particular by the religiously inspired one. The actual feelings and thinkings of a human being are not split, and poets were the first to know and to express this fact. A man loves God spiritually but with a more or less decisive carnal overtone as is demonstrated by the torments of the mysticists who are just an extreme example of a common fact. The same man definitely claims in the secular realm of love a spiritual complement. He refuses, in general at least, to totally identify love with sexuality. But the complexity of the secularization of the religious vocabulary does not stop here. Beside the psychologically rooted parallelism between religious/spiritual and secular love there is the fact that the Old Provençal poets, like most poets, acted as conscious creators, more and more aware of the aesthetic value of ambiguity. Looking for a certain effect, they "exaggerated" in their creative mood the secularization to a point where they founded a counter-religion: the totally secularized religion of love. At the same time, they were successful, by the very use of a religiously-tinged vocabulary and of religious themes (cf. next chapt.), in not provoking too sharply the Church which was more inclined to be more lenient towards a metaphoric expression of profane love than towards earthly crudities. Guillaume IX, of course, could not have cared less about this type of preoccupation. Yet, even his vocabulary is loaded with religious allusions and ornements. After what we said, this should not surprise us.

Chapter V

THE THEMES OF *CORTEZIA*

The language of the troubadours is so rich in themes that we have only attempted here to discuss a small number of them which are of religious origin or which reveal religious tendencies. The following areas are considered: love as a civilizing power and the source of all virtues, the theme of mercy, *joy* as a theme, the commandments of love, the beginnings of a true religion of love, various themes of religious origin, the martyrdom of love, and mystical elements.

1. *Love as a civilizing power and the source of all virtues*

Köhler says in one of his articles: "Love as a civilizing power [...] is the great discovery of the troubadours." [1] It may be asked whether a passage from the Gospel according to St. John may not have served as a model: John I, 4-7: "Deus charitas est," which may have been mentally transposed into "Deus amor est." Earthly love is in any case idealized to the level of a moralizing force.

Example: Bernard de Ventadour, *Ges de chantar no·m pren talans* (ed. Lazar, 11, 25-28, p. 100):

> Per re nom es om tan prezans
> Com per amor e per domnei

---

[1] Köhler, Erich, *Ideal und Wirklichkeit in der höfischen Epik*, Beiheft 97 zur *Zeitschrift für Romanische Philologie*, Tübingen, 1956, p. 141.

> Que d'aqui mou deportz e chans
> E tot can a proez'abau.

(Through nothing is man so gallant as through love and service of a lady, for out of these come joy, singing and everything belonging to prowess.)

Id., Lancan folhon bosc e jarric (ed. Lazar, 6, 17-18, p. 82):

> Ben a mauvais cor a mendic
> Qui ama e no·s melhura;

(That man has certainly a bad and vile heart, who loves and does not improve himself.)

For Gaucelm Faidit, love is the source of all virtues: *Tug cilh que amon valor* (ed. Raynouard, VI, 1-6, p. 295):

> Tug cilh que amon valor
> Devon saber que d'amor
> Mov larguez'e guais solatz,
> Franchez'et humilitatz,
> Pretz d'amar, servirs d'onor,
> Gen teners, jois, cortezia;

(All who like worth ought to know that from love originate largesse and joyous bliss, sincerity and humility, the prestige of love, submission in love, tender affection, joy, courtliness.)

The unpredictable Guillaume IX can also see an occasional bad influence in love, *Mout jauzens me prenc en amar* (ed. Jeanroy, IX, 27-30, p. 23):
Love (joy) can:

> E savis hom enfolezir
> E belhs hom sa beutat mudar
> E·l plus cortes vilanejar
> E totz vilas encortezir.

(... cause the wisest man to become deranged, the most handsome to lose his handsomeness, the most courtly to become common and the most common to become courtly.)

As a realist, Guillaume recognizes the negative aspects of love, which can throw the strongest man off balance. The idealizing tendency is secondary for the Aquitanian prince.

In a *Partimen*, a certain Guigo debates with a certain Bernard [2] concerning the loftier values possessed by military service and by the service of love:

> Guigo, ges tan no pot poiar
> En pretz cavalliers per razo
> Per armas cum per dompnejar;
> Quar dona·l fai valent e pro,
> Larc e ardit e de belle paria
> Et armas brau, felh e de maltalan

(Guigo, a knight, can certainly not rise as high in virtue trough arms as through the service of love; for the lady makes him into an excellent, courageous, generous, bold and sociable person, but arms make him coarse, deceitful and ill-tempered.)

One could multiply examples at will to indicate how love raises man to an ethically higher position. [3]

2. *The theme of mercy*

In the chapter on vocabulary the close relationships between mercy and compassion were pointed out. *Clamar merce*, "to beg for mercy," belongs to the classical period of the *canso*, from which time it slipped into the status of a cliché. Attempts have already been made to explain the expression by reference to the formula *criar merce* belonging to the language of the tournament and by which the vanquished asked the victor for mercy. Scheludko answers the problem with a psychological argument: "The request for mercy presumes the consciousness of guilt, which in no way

---

[2] Quoted by Kolsen, *Studi Medievali*, XII, 1939, p. 189.
[3] Cf. Denomy, "Courtly Love and Courtliness," *Speculum*, XXVIII, 1953, pp. 44-63; Pollmann, L., *op. cit.*, pp. 137 sq., suggests the troubadours "bestow the affirmed profane love with the dimension of an ideology" (p. 219).

belongs to the normal circumstances." [4] He has no doubt in mind that *merces* is taken directly from the sphere of religion. *Clamar merce* did not become a conventional secular theme until the later period of the troubadour development, e.g. in Bernart Marti and particulary in Arnaut Maruelh. From then on the theme became a *locus communis*.

Merces is frequently found used consciously in the religious sense. Along with *dreit*, "justice and compassion," it is one of the most common attributes of God. *Dreit* and *merces* are not mutually exclusive, but even in the theological sense, a nuance of differentiation slipped in, which the troubadours were quick to seize upon.

Arnaut de Maruelh, *A gran:*

> No m'en val razos
> Mas chauzimens e merces e perdos [5]

(Right is no help to me, but only clemency, mercy and forgiveness.)

Peire Vidal, *Tant ai longamen cercat* (ed. Anglade, X, 85, p. 29) uses a metaphor *oils de merce, boca de chauzimen*, "eyes of mercy, mouth of grace," which corresponds to an attribute of the Virgin (cf. the section on the Virgin Mary). His worshipping of his lady is clearly of religious character (ed. Anglade, X, 27-28 and 87-90):

> Eu clam merce a merces no·m socor;
> Merce claman cug morir de dolor.
> ....
> Per qu'eu ai mes en vos ferm'esperansa
> Et tot mon cor et tota ma fiansa,
> E fatz de vos ma domn'e mon senhor
> E·us ren mon cor de bon cor e d'amor.

(I beg mercy, but mercy does not help me; begging mercy I think I die of pain. [...] For it is in you that I placed my firm hope and all my heart and all my trust; I made of you my lady and my lord and I gladly submit my heart to you in love.)

---

[4] Scheludko, D., "Religöse Elemente...," p. 415.
[5] Quoted by Scheludko, "Religöse Elemente...," p. 417.

Other examples: Giraut de Bornelh, *Quan lo freitz e·l glatz e la neus* (ed. Berry, *Florilèges*, p. 216):

> Aissi·us clam merce humilmens,
> Bona domna et avinens.

> (And so I supplicate humbly your mercy, fair and outstanding lady.)

We can hear a real cry of despair in Bernard de Ventadour, *Pois preyatz me, senhor* (ed. Lazar, 18, 46-49, p. 130):

> Bona domna, merce
> Del vostre fin aman!
> Mas jonchas, ab col cle,
> Vos m'autrei e·m coman.

> (Good lady, mercy on your true lover! With clasped hands and inclined head I concede and request your protection.)

No transgression is serious enough to make forgiveness impossible. This concept forming another part of the theme of mercy/compassion echoes the infinite compassion of God. Peire Vidal, *Nuls hom no·s pot d'amor gandir* (ed. Anglade, XXV, 37-38, p. 81):

> [...] Pietatz
> Dezencolpa·ls plus encolpatz.

> (Poety can absolve even the most guilty of their sins.)

3. *The theme of joy*

Joy is an "exaltation intérieure,"[6] and "état d'esprit qui élève l'homme au-dessus de lui-même."[7] Marcabru says in one of his poems (ed. Dejeanne, *Poésies complètes du troubadour Marcabru*, Toulouse, 1909, XXXVII, 6):

---

[6] Frappier, J., *op. cit.*, p. 140.
[7] Jeanroy, A., *La poésie lyrique des Troubadours*, I, p. 74.

> Amors
> Es de joi cim'e racina
>
> (Love is the peak and the root of joy.)

The personification of abstract notions is rather infrequent in Classical Latin but very common in Biblical language and throughout the Middle Ages.[8] *Joy* is already used frequently as a concrete noun by Guillaume IX. Then Marcabru especially developed *joy* into a theme. It is however something of an exaggeration to say that he popularized it (Errante), since its popularity among the broad public is relatively insignificant in comparison to other themes. Marcabru's battles between personified vices and virtues undoubtedly influenced the initiated group of poets, without being taken up enthusiastically by the general public. Spitzer comments:

> *Joi*, ce mot si essentiel dans la poésie troubadourique, est d'abord la vraie joie dans sa plénitude, immaculée, la joie (*gaudium, delectatio* des Pères de l'Eglise) du chrétien qui a choisi raisonnablement la voie du Salut, de ce *bonus amor* (Saint Augustin: *Recta itaque voluntas est bonus amor, et voluntas perversa malus amor* [...]), qui sera récompensé un jour par la vision céleste, au Paradis, de Dieu. [...] *Joi* est ensuite la joie d'amour, toute morale elle aussi, bien que transposée sur le plan humain, puisqu'émanant de la dame, et c'est cette *joie* émanant du couple vertueux qui rayonnera à la fin de l'*Erec* de Chrétien sur toute la cour, qui sera la *Saelde* des *Minnesänger* allemands, faite de vertus et de plaisir.[9]

One of the original sources may perhaps be found in Romans 14, 17: "Regnum Dei est gaudium in Spirito Sancto." Joy can become the direct object of reverence in a hymn, as we have already seen in the "Joy of joys" of St. Augustine. Similarly in Peire Vidal, *Be m'agrada la covinens sazos* (ed. Anglade, XXVII, 41-42, p. 88):

---

[8] Scheludko, D., *op. cit.*, p. 408.

[9] Spitzer, Leo, "L'amour lointain de Jaufré Rudel et le sens de la poesie des troubadours," *Romanische Literaturstudien*, Tübingen, p. 310.

> Fis gaugz entiers placens amoros
> Ab vos es gaugz per que totz bes reviu.

(Perfect, unlimited joy, sweet pleasure of love, this happines is [connected] with you, through which all good things are reborn.)

Joi often develops into a borderline theme, that is, it partially overlaps into the sphere of mysticism. The adoration expressed through hymns, with which *joi* was associated, already indicates this passage; but even more it is felt in an experience which penetrates to the very roots of the poetic personality, in which joy floods over the poet with the same intensity as the Holy Spirit descends onto the enlightened soul. *Joi* is here very close to the highly-prized *laetitia* of the mystics: Jaufré Rudel, *No sap chantar qui so non di* (ed. Jeanroy, VI, 13, p. 16):

> Colps de joy me fer, que m'ausi

(I was struck by a blow of joy, which killed me.)

4. *Praise of the lady*

The eulogy is a literary commonplace in medieval writing. The *canso* too has recourse to the encomiastic mode, that is, it is clothed in the form of a eulogy: Guillaume IX, *Mout jauzens me prenc en amar* (ed. Jeanroy, IX, 37-42, p. 23-24):

> Si·m vol mi dons s'amor donar,
> Pres suy del penr' e del gazir
> E del celar e del blandir
> E de sos plazers dir e far
> E de sos pretz tener en car
> E de son laus enavantir.

(If my lady wishes to give me her love, I am ready to take it and to thank her, ready to hide it and to court her, ready to talk and to act in order to please her, ready to appreciate her merit and to promote her eulogy.)

The protestation of love is completely mixed with the praise of the perfect lady. The eulogy is already found in Arabic-Oriental lyrics, from which fact it was too hastily concluded that the true source had been discovered. But Scheludko dismisses this possibility somewhat too readily. His only argument against Arabic influence is an unsupported declaration: "The connection with Arabic literature remains an entirely ungrounded supposition." [10] The works of Nykl and Briffault do however offer a number of important documents which must be taken into consideration. Attempts have also been made to explain the encomiastic tendencies of the *canso* in sociological terms, in connection with the feudal relationships (e.g. Wechssler, *Das Kulturproblem des Minnesangs*). Finally, in his *Entstehungsgeschichte des provenzalischen Minnesangs*, Brinkmann traces them back to the widespread panegyric poetry in honour of prominent ladies. Neither of these two explanations should be simply rejected or qualified as "idle." [11] Pointing out that Guillaume was no poet-singer, "but one of the most powerful sovereigns of the Occident," [12] is not a sound enough argument to prove that the feudal system and its concepts did not help to colour the works of Guillaume and his aristocratic and non-aristocratic successors. Peire Vidal says, for example in *Ges pel temps fer e brau* (ed. Anglade, XXIII, 21-28, p. 72-73):

> De lai on venh ni vau,
> Sui vostres bendizens
> E sers obediens,
> Com cel qu·ab vos estau,
> Per far vostres talens;
> E ja·l francs jauzimens
> No·m deuria tarzar
> So que·m fai esperar:

(From wherever I come, to wherever I go, I praise you properly, for I am with you in order to carry out your will; your noble indulgence should not make me wait anymore fort what I am hoping.)

Bernard de Ventadour, *Pel doutz chan que·l rossinhols fai* (ed. Lazar, 10, 29-32, p. 98):

---

[10] Scheludko, D., *op. cit.*, p. 19.
[11] *Ibid.*
[12] *Ibid.*

> Domna, vostre sui e serai,
> Del vostre servizi garnitz.
> Vostr' om sui juratz e plevitz,
> E vostre m'era des abans.

> (Lady, I am yours and will be yours, I am ready to serve you. I am your totally devoted and liege man, and I was always yours.)

Many other troubadours use this same or a similar expression *(om juratz e plevitz, om liges)*, i.e. the religiously-tinged vocabulary of the vassalage.

Let it be stated once more that no single source should be regarded as excluding all others. This is of course just as true in the case of the many parellels that may be seen between secular lyrics and religious writings; one is justified only in calling them very important spheres of influence. The religious element is only one of many.

Obedience *(obediensa)*, adoration *(venerazio)*, love of God, faithfulness, humility *(umilitatz)* are all stimuli which invite the man to a eulogy concerning the object of his veneration. The Bible, and particularly the Psalms, show dozens of examples. The *laudes* were inserted into the liturgy and entered into the *matutinae laudes* as psalms of praise. Scheludko comments: "The theme of praise was transformed into an indispensable trait of Christian hymnody."[13] The hymns started out with words like *Ad Christi laudem virginis....*

Examples:

A eulogy of a lady consisting of the traditional elements is further enhanced by the regal quality of the introduction: Peire Vidal *Car' amiga douss'e Franca* (ed. Anglade, VI, 22-24, p. 14):

> Sobeirana
> De joi e de benestansa
> E de valor e d'onransa.

> (Queen of joy and perfection, of worth and honour.)

---

[13] Scheludko, D., *op. cit.*, p. 20.

The eulogy is sometimes carried to the point of comparing the lady to God. The comparison works out in her favour. Peire Vidal, *En un terra estranha* (ed. Anglade, VIII, 61-65, p. 22):

> Domna, Deus qu'es leials e vers
> Vos a dat pretz, honor e be
> Pro mais que no·n retenc ab se.
> Que mainta gens ditz de vos be,
> Que luy renega e mescre.

> (Lady, God who is honourable and just has granted you worth, honour, and material things far in excess of what He has retained for Himself. For many people speak highly of you, who refuse to believe in Him.)

5. *The theme of the Virgin Mary*

Many expressions of homage contain attributes that are otherwise applied to the Mother of Christ. Especially popular is a whole series of personified abstractions, which are similar in their affectation; e.g.: "river of bliss," "source of mercy," "fruit of joy," "flower of beauty," etc. Such figures of speech may be traced back to the Christian Greek literature, and even further back to the flowery language of the Oriental poets, especially those who worshipped Mary in the early days of Christianity. But at first the religious symbolism connected with Mary was in general rather modest. Then, around the beginning of the twelfth century, it reached its first high point of development in the Latin hymns to the Virgin. The variations become innumerable in the thirteenth century. Mariolatry and idolatry of the woman complemented each other mutually. Toward the end of the twelfth century there are signs that many of the troubadours' appellatives are being borrowed from those applied to the Virgin: the sun, the rose, the spring-flower, the mirror of love, *miralh d'amor* (the mirror theme alone would offer sufficient material for a specialized study, particularly from the psychological point of view). In the hymns sung to the Virgin we find *speculum paradisi;* in the secular *canso, claus de bon pretz* ("the key to true perfection") corresponds to *clavis regni caelistis* in the hymns to Mary.

Youth is celebrated in the secular lyric: *capduelh de joven;* in the hymns to the Virgin: *dux animorum.* The example "peak and root of joy, of virtue" has already been mentioned; the hymns to the Virgin include: *radix gratiae, innocentiae, pudentiae. Combra de joi* corresponds to *domus laetitia,* etc.[14]

Of particular significance is the wealth of conventional imagery in Peire Vidal, *Car amiga douss' e Franca* (ed. Anglade, VI, 9-12 and 18-20, p. 13-14):

> Quar vos etz arbres e branca
> On fruitz de gaug s'assazona
> Pero qui a vos s'adona
> No tem folzer ni lavanca.
> ....
> Fina beutatz vos faissona
> Ad ops de portar corona
> Sus en l'emperial banca.

(For you are the tree and the branch on which ripens the fruit of joy. He who dedicated himself to you has no fear of lightning or avalanche. [...] Perfect beauty adorns you, so that you may wear the crown on the imperial throne.)

In the hymns to the Virgin, "fruit of joy" designates Christ: "Benedictus fructus quem peperit Mariae."[15]

In general it may be said that as far as the theme of the Virgin is concerned, there is mutual influence from both sides. The great development of hymns to the Virgin does not take place until the thirteenth century, and it is difficult, if not impossible, to decide to what extent the religious elements influenced the secular, and vice versa.

6. *The commandments of love*

The fruits of love can never be plucked if the lover does not begin by submitting absolutely to the commandments of the lady.

---

[14] These are epithets used by A. de Maruelh, quoted in Scheludko, "Beiträge...," p. 194.
[15] cf. Scheludko, D. "Religiöse Elemente...," p. 26.

This act, demanding a great deal of self-control, even to the point of self-denial, calls to mind the overcoming of *superbia* which is demanded of the philosopher as well as the Christian. At the same time, the lover hoped that through his sacrifice (another concept of religious origin) he would be able to climb higher up the ladder of virtue. Even the sacrifices demanded of the supposedly selfless lover show partial influence from the notions of mysticism, as, for example, in the required denial of personal will and freedom which threaten to stand in the way of any *unio*.

Guillaume IX already expressed this demand in precise terms, *Pus vezem de novelh florir* (ed. Jeanroy, VII, 25-26, p. 18):

> Ja no sera nuils hom ben fis
> Contr'amor si non l'es aclis
>
> (No one may be assured of being a servant of love if he does not entirely submit to its will.)

Earthly pleasures must turn toward humility, when the lady reveals her qualities. Here too, Guillaume furnishes an example, *Mout jauzens me prenc en amar* (ed. Jeanroy, IX, 19-21, p. 22-23):

> Totz joys li deu humiliar
> Et totz ricor obezir
> Mi dons
>
> (All [other, earthly] joy must fade to insignificance before her, and every noble owes my lady obedience.)

With the help of religious vocabulary (*humiliar, obezir*), a nuance is added to the word *joy*. No earthly pleasures can compare with the joy that love has the power to grant. Thus, as early as Guillaume IX, *joy d'amor* is raised to a sort of extraterrestrial sphere. This impression is strengthened still further by the fact that the use of *mi dons* for "my lady," although traditional, would have a memory association with the cry "my God."

Subjection can also bring suffering: Peire Vidal, *Ges del joi que ai no·m rancur* (ed. Anglade, III, 12-13, p. 6):

> Qu'on plus li sui humilians,
> Adoncs me dona plus d'esglai.

> (The more I humble myself before her, the more pain she causes me.)

The following quotation may perhaps be connected with the Biblical "He who humbles himself shall be raised up"; Giraut de Bornelh (ed. Kolsen, XLV, 82):

> Per c'umiliatz
> Val las conoissens
>
> (Humility helps the clever man.)

Like all qualities of the lady, *umiliatz* has the power to elevate the lover morally, even more sometimes than the other attributes. Peire Vidal, *Son ben apoderatz* (ed. Anglade, XV, 68-70, p. 46):

> Ai! Don, humilitatz
> E pretz e pietatz
> Vos met'entre mos bratz.
>
> (Ah, lady, may humility, worth and pity place you in my arms.)

The idea of subjection was also influenced by the feudal system. The lover was elevated by the lady to the position of a vassal of love. The creation of a vassal relationship took place in a three-step ceremony:

1. the oath of fidelity
2. the *immixtio manuum* (placing of the folded hands in those of the lord, who closes his over them.)
3. *osculum* (the kiss following the pledge of loyalty.)

At the very least it may be assumed that the *hommage féodal* served as a model for the *hommage amoureux* as, for example, in the humble attitude of the lover kneeling before his lady: Bernard de Ventadour, *Lancan vei per mei la landa* (ed. Lazar, 29, 29-35, p. 172-174):

> Mal o fara, si no·m manda
> Venir lai on se despolha,
> Qu'eu sia per sa comanda,
> Pres del leih, josta l'esponda,
> E·lh traya·ls sotlars ne chaussans,

> A genolhs et umilians,
> Si·lh platz que sos pes me tenda.

(She would do wrong were she not to bid me come there where she undresses in order that I might be at her service near her bed, beside the bedstead, and that on my knees and humbly I might draw off her well-fitting shoes if she deigns to stretch out her feet to me.) [16]

7. *The beginnings of a true religion of love*

In the conscious use of theologically-inspired vocabulary, it is easy to relate the adoration of the lady and the worship of God through a few parallels. Once again the transcendental conception of love is foreshadowed in the poems of Guillaume IX. The lover has prospects of attaining a sort of Paradise of love (it can be found poetically wherever the lady is) if he lives according to the laws of love: *Pus vezem de novelh florir* (ed. Jeanroy, VII, 11-12, p. 17):

> Pero Ieumens
> Dona gran joy qui be·n mante
> Los aizimens.

(But I know that it [love] grants great joy to whoever lives according to its laws.)

For Bernard de Ventadour, *Can la freid'aura venta* (ed. Lazar, 26, 3-5, p. 160), the country of the lady corresponds to Paradise:

> Veyaire m'es qu'eu senta
> Un ven de paradis
> Per amor de la genta.

(It seems to me that I detect a breeze out of paradise because of my love for a noble lady.)

---

[16] Translated by Denomy, *art. cit., Med. Stud.*, VII, 1945, p. 169. This passage is a good example of what might be called *meridional libertinage*. The intention is obviously profane, the style, at the climax of this dramatically structured poem, uses religious terms and pictures.

See also *Gent estera que chantes* (ed. Lazar, 37, strophe IV, p. 202-203). In *Tant ai mo cor ple de joya* (ed. Lazar, 4, 57-58, p. 74) Bernard de Ventadour takes the pose of the humble prayer:

> Domna, per vostr'amor
> Jonh las mas et ador!

(Lady, for your love I clasp my hands and adore you!)

The same poet implores his lady just as he begs God for mercy: *Ara no vei luzir solelh* (ed. Lazar, 5, 54-56, p. 80):

> Ai, domna, per merce·us playa
> C'ayatz de vostr' amic merci,
> Pus aitan gen vos merceya.

(Ah, lady, for mercy's sake, may you please feel pity for your lover since he is gently imploring your compassion).

The urge toward withdrawal from the world which was taken up in religious spheres by the monastic orders finds similar expression in the secular lyric; Giraut de Bornelh (ed. Kolsen, VIII, 52):

> Tan es rich'e pros a valens
> Cela de cui eu sui rendutz

(So noble and virtuous and excellent is the one into whose orders I have entered.)

In Old Provençal, *rendre* means "to enter a monastery." *Id.* (XII, 9):

> La bela cui sui profers

(The beautiful one to whom I have given my oath.)

Profer may be understood in the sense of "qui a fait profession." Guillaume IX, *Farai chansoneta nueva* (ed. Jeanroy, IX, 25-26, p. 21):

> Qual pro y auretz, s'ieu m'enclostre
> E no·m retenez per vostre?

(How will you benefit if I withdraw from the world and if you do not hold me back to be yours?)

The feeling of guilt has already been mentioned. Many troubadours desire consciously to do penance, modeling their attitudes on the Biblical situations of penitent sinners, as in Zorzi, *Aissi:* [17]

> Estai penedens et confes

Paraphrases are also found: consider, for example, the words "Forgive them for they know not what they do": Peire Vidal, *Tant ai longamen cercat* (ed. Anglade, X, 59-60, p. 28):

> Mas deu m'esser perdonat,
> Que no sai que·m dia.

> (But I have to be forgiven, for I do not know what I say.)

Bernard de Ventadour, *Lo tems vai e ven e vire* (ed. Lazar, 44, 31-32, p. 232):

> Qui vid anc mais penedensa
> Faire denan lo pechat?

Thus the new religion acknowledges its sins: Peire Vidal, *Bels amics cars, ven s'en vas vos estius* (ed. Anglade, IV, 35, p. 10):

> Grans peccatz es, si.m torn'en nonchaler.

> (It is a grave sin [deadly sin], if she remains cold toward me.)

We can recognize an ambivalent urge toward salvation in the following lines of Vidal, which seem to invite a modern existentialist interpretation. *Car' amiga, douss'e Franca* (ed. Anglade, VI, 31-32, p. 13):

> Per c'om deu cercar garensa,
> Ans que torn'en decadensa.

---

[17] Quoted by Scheludko, "Religiöse Elemente...," p. 28.

THE THEMES OF "CORTEZIA" 79

(Man must also seek his salvation before he gives himself over to destruction.)

The use of attributes of the Virgin Mary also is part of the attempt to create a religion of love: Peire Vidal, *Tant ai longamen cercat* (ed. Anglade, X, 85, p. 29):

> Olhs de merce, boca de chauzimen
>
> (Eyes of mercy, mouth of compassion.)

The lover formulates a prayer of love: Peire Vidal, *Son ben poderatz* (ed. Anglade, XV, 68-70, p. 46):

> Ai! Don, humilitatz
> E pretz e pietatz
> Vos met'entre mos bratz.
>
> (Ah, lady, may humility, worth and pity bring you into my arms.)

The sight of the beloved calls up the sight of God: In several of his poems, Peire Vidal invokes God in connexion with the beloved lady, and there are passages which border on blasphemy. Some examples: *Tant ai logamen cercat* (ed. Anglade, X, 24-36, p. 26):

> Qu'ab leis no trob amistat ni pitansa
> Ni clauzimen ni negun' acordansa;
> Eu clam merce e merces no·m socor;
> Merce claman cug morir de dolor.
>
> Tant clam ab humilitat
> Merce cascun dia,
> Merces faria peccat,
> Si no m'en valia.
> Mout ai chauzimen cridat
> Ves que pauc m'embria
> Pos ab leis non ai trobat,
> Eu cre que mortz sia.
>
> (With her I can find neither friendship nor pity, nor grace, nor any acquiescence at all. I claim mercy but mercy does not help me; crying for mercy I think I will die of pain. I beg for mercy every day with so much humility that mercy would commit a sin if it would not

assist me. I have asked for mercy for a long time, but it was of little help to me. Since I did not find it, I think it is dead.)

Mout m'es bon e bel (ed. Anglade, XVIII, 41-45, p. 53):

> Que per amador
> Mi ten com lo seu,
> E prec la per Deu
> Qu'ilh esgart com eu
> L'aurai estat de bon sen,

(For she has accepted me as her lover, and I beg her through God to observe how faithful I was to her.)

Estat ai gran sazo (ed. Anglade, XXXIV, 31-40, p. 109):

> Domna, per Deu del tro,
> Pos aissi·m rent a vos,
> Humils e volontos,
> Vostr'amistat me do
> Chauzimens e merces
> E precs e bona fes;
> E faretz vostr'onor:
> Que mout ai gran paor
> Que·l talans m'apoder,
> A cui no·m posc tener.

(Lady, by God of Heaven, since I surrender myself to you in such a humble and voluntary manner, may your grace and mercy grant your friendship to my prayers and my good faith; it will be to your honor: for I am very much frightened to be overwhelmed by the desire which I am not able to resist.)

Quant hom es en autrui poder (ed. Anglade, XXXIX, 41-42, p. 124):

> Bona dompna, Deu cug vezer,
> Quam lo vostre gen cors remir:

(Good lady, I have the impression of seeing God when I glance at your graceful body.) [18]

---

[18] When the troubadours refer in their love lyrics to God, "invariably their references are to our minds shocking and irreverent." (Cf. Denomy, *art. cit.*, p. 181.)

Raimon Jordan (ed. Hilding Kjellmann, *Le Troubadour Raimon-Jordan,* Upsala, 1922, XIII, pp. 46-54) goes as far as placing a night with his beloved above paradise:

> E s'eu en dic mon conort,
> No m'o tengatz ad orgolh,
> Que tan la desir e volh
> Que, s'er'en coita de mort,
> Non queri a Deu tan fort
> Que lai el seu paradis
>   M'aculhis
> Lom que'm des lezer
> D'una noit ab leis jazer.

(And if I tell you the joy I have of her, do not hold it against me as a prideful thing, because so much do I desire her and want her that, if I were in danger of death, even then I would not so strongly beg God to receive me in His Paradise as I do beg Him to grant me the opportunity of lying one night with her. [Transl. by Denomy, *art. cit.*, p. 182.])

The pilgrim of the faith is at the same time a pilgrim of love: Jaufré Rudel, *Lanquan li jorn son lonc en may* (ed. Jeanroy, V, 12-14, p. 13):

> Ai! car me fos lai pelegris
> Si que mos fustz e mos tapis
> Fos pels sieus belhs huelhs ramiratz!

(Ah! if only I were a pilgrim there so that my staff and cloak might be admired by her beautiful eyes!)

A disquieting figure in the *canso* is that of the *lauzengier,* the person who constantly spoils the plans of the longing, pure-hearted lover, and who is generally jealous as well. Often the husband is meant. Could he not be thought of as a symbol of Lucifer, who tarnishes the pure relationship of the lover to his lady through his demands for carnal possession?

We are purposely limiting the discussion here to the "beginnings of a religion of love." The troubadours shied away from setting up any decipherable theory or any system or dogma they stayed rather between the religious and the secular, and realized also the attractiveness of such a viewpoint.

It is often the case that lyrical effusion within the *canso* is akin to a confession or reveals autobiographical traits. But this is not personal poetry in the true sense of the word. "The love of the troubadours is not related to experience [Erlebnis] but to value," [19] says Pollmann. It can be shown that the Old Provençal poets have firm roots within liturgical traditions as far as form is concerned, but that they maintain a considerable distance from the actual content of the theme, which may be expressed, for example, in a sudden reversal into the ironic mode (irony toward themselves or toward the lady). They use self-abasement and humility as a vehicle to help them reach their goals, goals which do not perhaps go beyond literary ambitions.

8. *Various themes of religious origin*

In this section are placed Biblical themes, direct borrowing from Biblical texts, paraphrases and parodies. *Joy* can represent something extraterrestrial and be as incomparable as the joy in Paradise coming from contemplation of the face of God: Guillaume IX, *Mout jauzens me prenc en amar* (ed. Jeanroy, IX, 16-18, p. 22), a hymn to joy:

> Aitals joys no pot par trobar
> E qui be·l volria lauzar
> D'un an no y poiri'parvenir.
>
> (Such joy cannot be equalled and whoever were to attempt to praise it adequately, would not succeed even if he spent a whole year on it.)

Many lines in the form of a prayer are to be found: Bernard de Ventadour, *Per melhs cobrir lo mal pes e·l cossire* (ed. Lazar, 21, 17, p. 140):

> E ren lor en laus e merces e gratz
>
> (Therefore I offer them praise, thanks and gratitude.)

---

[19] Pollmann, *op. cit.*, p. 139.

The absence of the lady reminds the poet of a time of penance and fasting; Bernard de Ventadour, *Amics Bernartz de Ventadorn* (ed. Lazar, 28, 40, p. 170):

> Faih ai lonja carantena
>
> (I have completed a long penance.)

Pity, the key to faith, becomes also the key to love: Bernard de Ventadour, *Non es meravelha s'eu chan* (ed. Lazar, 1, 23, p. 60):

> No pot claus obrir mas merces
>
> (No key can open [the prison] except pity.)

Direct borrowings from the morning hymns *(hymnis in matutinis laudibus)* are also found.[20] Giraut de Bornelh speaks of *reis glorios; verais lums et clartatz,* which corresponds to the parallelism God/light which can be seen in the morning hymns: "Deus qui caeli lumen est; aeterna lucis conditor; lux ipse totus; verum lumen," etc.

Mass was of course a living reality for all poets. Perhaps Bernard de Ventadour was thinking of the *mea culpa* as he wrote: *Conortz, era sai eu be* (ed. Lazar, 15, 17-18, p. 116):

> Per ma colpa m'esdeve
> Que ja no·n sia privatz,
>
> (It is my own fault that I am no longer her close friend.)

The Holy Scriptures are mentioned: Bernard de Ventadour, *Lo tems vai e ven e vire* (ed. Lazar, 44, 40-42, p. 234):

> Que se mostra l'escriptura:
> Causa de bon'aventura
> Val us sols jorns mais de cen.
>
> (For so the Holy Scriptures show: in the case of good fortune, a single day is worth more than a hundred.)

---

[20] Quoted in Scheludko, *Entstehungsgeschichte...*, p. 204.

Likewise the use of the brother figure in the sense of "fellow man" is of Biblical origin; Bernard de Ventadour, *Lo rossinhols s'ebaudeya* (ed. Lazar, 23, 31-32, p. 148):

> Mas ben es vertatz que laire
> Cuida, tuih sion sei fraire!

(But it is true that a thief thinks all men are his brothers.)

We find in Peire Vidal a parody of the apocalyptic judgement, where the good are rewarded and the bad are damned; *Be m'agrada la covinens sazos* (ed. Anglade, XXVII, 25-32, p. 87):

> Deus vos sal, domna, quar etz bel'e pros,
> Mas ja no sal cels que son mal mescliu,
> E Deus sal me, quar vas vos m'umiliu,
> Mas ges nos sal lauzengiers ni gilos.
> Deus sal los pros e·ls adregz e·ls prezatz,
> Mas ja no sal los enoios malvatz,
> Deus sal ottz drutz, quant amon finamen,
> Mas ja no sal cel qu'ad enoi s'empren.

(God save you, lady, for you are beautiful and noble, but may He damn the evil and envious; God save me, for I am humble toward you, but may He damn the slanderers and the jealous. God save the valiant, courtly and esteemed men, but may He damn the wicked and importunate; God save all pure-heated lovers, but may He damn anyone who compromises with boredom.)

The affectation displayed by many of the images used by the troubadours may be largely explained by reference to the language of the Scriptures. These represented for them "the most dependable treasure-house of poetic language."[21] Love lyrics offer us an amalgamation of secular/pagan and Christian/religious elements.

In addition to his neglect of the Arabic influence, which has already been mentioned, Scheludko unfortunately passes in silence over the possible influence of mysticism and its conception of

---

[21] Scheludko, D., "Religiöse Elemente...," p. 33.

love. The famous theme of the martyrdom of love leads us into the mystical element.

9. *The martyrdom of love*

The troubadours are fond of dying of love in their poems. This readiness, even though it is only on paper, is clearly taken over from the religious model of the martyr's death. The legends of the saints were accepted in the twelfth and thirteenth centuries as being lively memories of events or even as absolute reality. Of course, hagiographical works are among the earliest products of Romance literature. Martyrdom does not necessarily imply death; it may also be limited to indescribable tortures: Gillaume IX, *Pus vezem de novelh florir* (ed. Jeanroy, VII, 23-24, p. 17):

> "A bon coratge bon poder
> Qui's ben suffrens."
>
> (True courage brings great power, if you know how to be patient.)

Peire Vidal, *Per melhs sofrir lo maltrait e l'afan* (ed. Anglade, XLI, 27-30, p. 131):

> E per s'amor sofri tan greu martire
> Que la dolors m'a ja del tot conquis
> E·l deziriers que m'aura tost aucis:
> Et a·n gran tort, mas eu non lo·i aus dire.
>
> (And for her love I put up with such intense pain that I am already conquered by grief as well as by desire which will have killed me soon. She is quite wrong, but I do not dare to tell her.)

Guillaume de Cabestanh: [22]

> ... plus greu martire
> Nuls home, de me, no sen.

---

[22] Quoted in Wechssler, p. 277.

Bernard de Ventadour, *Tant ai mo cor ple de joya* (ed. Lazar, 4, 75-76, p. 76):

> La pena e la dolor
> Que·n trac, e·l martire.
>
> (The pain and the grief and the torment I suffer for her.)

Id., Amors, enquera·us preyara (ed. Lazar, 12, 63-64, p. 106):

> C'aitan doloirozamen
> Viu com cel que mor en flama;
>
> (Since I live as painfully as the one who is dying in the flames.)

In order to understand the torments of love or the renouncing of earthly existence in favour of a higher ideal, we must reach back to a notion which belongs to the irrational part of man: *passio*.[23] For the Ancients, and partly into the early Middle Ages, *passio* (Greek πάδος) was understood as a passive emotion peculiar to man and similar to his instincts. This passivity is responsible for the fact that *passio*, in ethical terms, was neutral, that is, was considered to be neither a moral advantage nor disadvantage. Nonetheless, Plato's *Phaedrus* had already pointed out man's responsibility in the wonderful comparison of the passions to fiery horses which could be valuable or destructive in character, depending on the firm control maintained by the driver. It was particularly the Stoics who saw a constant source of *perturbatio* in the *passiones*. For many Christian authors, *passio* was a *concupiscentia carnis*. Writers in the mystic tradition also perceive positive aspects in the volcanically explosive passions. The Pseudo-Areopagita (a Neo-Platonic Christian of the fifth century who is supposed to have written down the thoughts of Dionysius Areopagita, the first bishop of Athens), for whom ἔρως and ἀγάπη were identical in theological usage, says, concerning the love of God: "The love of God is also ecstatic, lifting

---

[23] Cf. Auerbach, Erich, "Passio als Leidenschaft," *PMLA*, LV, 1941, *passim*.

man outside himself, not allowing the lovers to belong to themselves, but to the one they love." [24] St. Augustine, too, modifies the pejorative connotation of *passio* into "motus animi contra rationem." [25] In the hands of the Christian mystics, the passive emotion is transformed into an active one, culminating in the *gloriosa passio* of divine love. Eartly afflictions can turn into passions, for the love of God is a *motus animi* free from earthly limitations, for which man is ready to suffer anything, even death. The notions of "suffering" and "creative urge" are brought closer and closer together. The instruments and accompanying phenomena of *passio* are significant: *crux, vulnera, gladius,* etc.

The active element within this "blind" passion is therefore of Christian origin. Above all, the mystics liked to stress the positive side. Their originality in relation to the concepts held in Antiquity and the early Middle Ages, which may for the most part be traced back to Aristotle (in Aristotle πάδος is a category; even the eleven principles of Aquinates, the six *passiones concupiscibiles* and the five *passiones irrascibiles* go back in the final analysis to the Stagirite), resides in the fact that "the spontaneity and creative drive of love is ignited by 'passio'." [26] The value of *passio* tends more and more toward the positive, and its apotheosis can become the ecstasy of love. [27] The quality of the human soul was recognized as being potentially dynamic; the only thing that had to be done was to prepare and guide it toward an eventual fusion, the *unio mystica* with God. What could be easier than to transpose this fully developed spiritualization of *amor carnalis* with respect to God into human categories as well? It goes without saying, of course, that this attempted spiritualization of the love of a man for a woman must be understood in relative terms only. Auerbach's conclusions point in this same direction: "All of these theme are to be found [...] as we all know, in secular love-lyrics as well — at times so strongly expressed that one may wonder if it actually is still secular poetry." [28]

---

[24] Pseudo-Areopagita, Chapter IV, p. 105.
[25] Cf. Auerbach's discussion of this.
[26] Auerbach, E., *op. cit.*, p. 1189.
[27] The interpretation of the *passiones* as active forces was later fully developed by Rousseau, Shaftesbury and many others.
[28] Auerbach, E., *op. cit.*, p. 1190.

10. The possibilities of mystical influence

There are scholars who cite Guillaume IX as a perfect model in connection with mysticism and its influence (Bezzola, Lerch). [29] They claim that Guillaume wanted to combat the growing influence of the priest Robert d'Abrissel, founder of the order of Fontevrault. In his aversion to the *clerici,* who he felt were too alineated from wordly concerns, but who were gaining unexpected response even among the higher social classes (as, for example, Guillaume's wife, who is said to have taken the veil under Robert d'Abrissel's influence), they postulate that Guillaume attempted to oppose the divine mysticism with an earthly one, centering around the lady, and thus, that he created *amor cortes*. There is nothing surprising, of course, in the analogy drawn between the mysticism of God and the mysticism of the lady. [30]

The spread of mystical attitudes goes back to the primeval origins of religion itself. Although the actual mysticism of love undoubtedly reaches its highest development with Guinicelli and Dante, the troubadours are a very important link in a chain that for Christianity began with St. John and continued with the Pseudo-Areopagita and Plotinus. St. Augustine played the decisive rôle, providing the transition between Hellenistic paganism and early Christianity and thus furtherering the development of Christian mysticism. The alleged writings of Dionysius Aeropagita associates love with the elevation of the soul toward virtue (the *summum bonum* of Plato), the concept which played such an important rôle among the troubadours (cf. *joy,* amor and other terms):

---

[29] Lerch, E., *op. cit., passim* and Bezzola, R. R., *Romania,* April, 1940, *passim.* For the influence of Avicenna's mystical writings and of other Arabian sources, cf. Denomy, *art. cit.,* pp. 184-205, and "An Inquiry into the Origins of Courtly Love," *Mediaeval Studies,* VI, 1944, pp. 246-256.

[30] In his discussion of the Augustinian *caritas* system (*amor origino omnium bonum*), Pollmann mentions in connection with its *appetitus boni* Gregory the Great, Jean de Fécamp, Guillaume de St. Thierry and Bernard de Clairvaux, i.e. the most famous mystics of the twelfth century. Cf. *op. cit.,* p. 224 and pp. 232 sq.

But why speak the Sacred Writers of God sometimes as ἔρως or ἀγάπη sometimes as Yearning and Love? In the one case He is the Cause and Producer and Begetter of the thing signified, int he other He is the thing signified Itself. Now the reason why He is Himself on the one hand moved by the quality signified, and on the other causes motion by it, is that He moves and leads onward Himself unto Himself. Therefore on the one hand they call Him the Object of Love and Yearning as being Beautiful and Good, and on the other they call Him Yearning and Love as being a Motive-Power leading all things to Himself, Who is the only ultimate Beautiful and Good-yea, as being His own Self-Revelation and the Bounteous Emanation of His own Transcendent Unity, a Motion of Yearning simple, self-moved, self-acting, pre-existent in the Good, and overflowing from the Good into creation, and once again returning to the Good. And herein the Divine Yearning, showeth especially its beginningless and endless nature, revolving in a perpetual circle for the Good, from the Good, in the Good, and to the Good, with unerring revolution, never varying its centre or direction, perpetually advancing and remaining and returning to Itself. This by Divine inspiration our renowned Initiator hath declared in his *Hymns of Yearning*, which it will not be amiss to quote and thus to bring unto a holy consummation our Discourse concerning this matter. [31]

The *unio mystica* goes back to Plato's theory of ideas, or at least to Plotinus' reworking of it: "But the former itself is *One-All*, for it is the first cause; the Cause is truly one. But that which comes after the first cause, because the One seems to weigh on it in this fashion, is everything which forms a part of the One, and also any portion whatever is *All and One*." [32] The passage quoted may also serve as a source of modern pantheism. In the classical period of the Middle Ages, mystical thought became unusually vigorous. The three main names to mention are: Jean de Fécamp, Bernard de Clairvaux and Hugues de St. Victor. But this revival of mysticism was not only of a theoretical nature; it was manifested as well in the wide acceptance of the principle

---

[31] Pseudo-Areopagita, Chapter IV, Paragraph 14, pp. 106-107.
[32] Plotinus, *One and Many*, 49 (102-106).

of the crusade. Sybel says in his *Geschichte des ersten Kreuzzuges:* "We see the lay people, folk of practical secular background, seized by the mystical appeal, as well as the monks, hermits and theologians." [33] Mysticism was not thought of first of all as an attitude toward life but as a means of drawing closer to one's beginnings and thereby to God. The troubadours must have found stimulation in it, which influenced their concepts of love. The piety of heart, appealing to the personal capacity for inspiration, offered the poets a new field which allowed them to give somewhat freer rein to their strongly subjective inclinations (cf. *Historical Outline*). [34] The mysticism of St. Bernard, which grew out of Augustine, scarcely makes any distinction between *amor* and *caritas,* just as the Pseudo-Areopagita had treated ἔρως and ἀγάπη as synonyms. The troubadours had a ready ear for such a combination of spiritual and sensual notions, because not only their vocabulary but also their themes are largely ambiguous. Their intangibility is not the least of the charms of the troubadour lyrics, and it dooms to failure any attempt to crystallize the essential quality of their conception of love. Such an ambivalent body of poetry could not long remain in its precarious position. The lyrical cult of the Virgin in the thirteenth century furnished the "necessary" framework, that is, it gave the impression of setting things back in their proper places, although it was itself strongly influenced by secular lyrics. These developments must therefore have been to a certain extent parallel. The glorification of pure love for a lady in extraterrestrial terms became a literary form, in time, a cliché, and was eventually enriched by one more element: The intellectual attitudes of Platonism and

---

[33] Quoted in Wechssler, *op. cit.,* p. 242.

[34] "In truth," comments Denomy, "it is difficult to reconcile Marcabru's expressions concerning *fin'amors* with divine love: the love of God, for example, is hardly a matter of self-promise and a pledge as *Amor* is; nor is its birth confined to the well-born and its growth to a leafy bower protected from the cold and the heat; nor, like *fin'amors,* does charity single out or reject an individual, nor is it fearful to boast of its possession becauses of the possibility of loss thereby. *Amors, fin'amors, bon'amors* is neither *caritas,* platonic love, nor purely carnal love or lust. It is a special type of love peculiar to the troubadours by whom, as far as historical texts allow us to know, it was formed, developed and spread." (" *Fin'Amors:* the Pure Love...," pp. 147-48.)

mysticism were firmly rooted in traditional learning up to the classical medieval period, but the fourteenth and fifteenth centuries witnessed a true rebirth of Plato. Beginning with Guinicelli and Dante, through Petrarch and his disciples, Marot, Marguerite de Navarre, Ronsard, and the Romantics, a line may be drawn indicating the continuation in literary terms of the Platonic heritage, alongside the purely philosophical tradition.

Bernard's concept of existence is contained in the treatise *De diligendo Deo* (about 1126).[35] The uniderlying principle is: "Causa diligendo Deus est, modus sine modo diligere." Lot-Borodine, with Gilson, one of the few scholars to investigate seriously the influence of mysticism, discovers in Bernard de Clairvaux four stages in the development of love:

1. Homo diligit se ipse propter se ipsum.
2. Amat iam Deum, sed propter se non propter ipsum.
3. Deum homo diligit, non propter se tantum, sed et propter ipsum.
4. Nec sed ipsum diligit homo, nisi propter Deo.[36]

Egoistical love is the starting point of Bernard's mysticism. Once more it is demonstrated thet the upholders of piety were particularly keen psychologial observers. In time, that is, with increasing maturity, the pure love of God develops after man has first loved Him for his own advantage. In the final step, man *is* love and lives according to the dictum: "Verus amor se ipso contentus est: habet praemium sed in quod amatur," which must have been very close to the conception of love held by most of the troubadours. Even this type of love, which is still comprehensible to the intellect, can be elevated until it merges in ecstatic union whit the object of love, which is required of the true *unio mystica*. To a certain extent this is an anticipation of the modern existentialist attempt to overcome the subject/object split. After attaining *unio,* the soul cries out: "O amor sanctus et castus! ô dulcis et suivis affectiao, ô pura et defaecata intentio voluntatis! ..." The words "intentio voluntatis" undoubtedly refer to lust.

---

[35] The following remarks are based partly on Lot-Borodine, *op. cit.,* pp. 229 sq.
[36] Quoted in Lot-Borodine, pp. 229-230.

Wechssler sees Christian mysticism as "the striving of the soul to escape the finite and its fusion with the infinite through the power of ecstatic love." [37]

The constant interchanging of terms such as *charitas, amor Dei, amor spiritualis, amor divinus, amor carnalis, amor mundi, cupiditas* was naturally a thorn in the side of the strict theologians. One of the troubadours attempted to fulfill the demands of theology for a clear differentiation between sensual and spiritual love: Marcabru. To what extent his dualistic system, which places *amor* (true love) in absolute opposition to *amar* (false love), was influenced by the Cathars or by Manichaeism cannot be dealt with here. [38] Although the theoreticians of the Church endeavoured, from the earliest times, to deepen the chasm separating the two types of love, the psychological principles which formed the basis for attempted explanations of the nature of all desires *(appetiti)* remained the same. Man was regarded as a whole and no longer as a good upper and a wicked lower half. The attitude was decisively established by the writings of the first great poet and psychologist of religion. "Augustine examined real man. He found that the basic form of the soul's activity lay in the striving for pleasure *(cupido, amor)*; no one could avoid this pattern. It was identical with the striving for possessions, for gratification.... All instincts are only derivations of this basic form, appearing sometimes more as an affectation, at other times more as an activity, and they are equally valid in the realm of sensual life." [39] Scholasticism does not yet differentiate the three independent areas in the life of the soul (thoughts, desires, feelings) but rather subordinates feelings to the will. Although the *appetitus* was considered by Augustine to be ethically neutral, the choice of his goals indicates that his attitude toward them was by no means neutral (cf. Plato's horses). According to the dualistic psychology of the will which grew out of these considerations, there were only the alternatives God/world, *charitas* or *cupiditas*.

---

[37] Wechssler, *op. cit.*, p. 243.
[38] Cf. Lazar, *op. cit.*, ch. II, pp. 47 sq., for a detailed discussion of the terms *fin'amors* and *fals'amors*.
[39] Harnack, G., *Lehrbuch der Dogmentgeschichte*, Berlin, 1885, III, p. 104.

It was soon recognized, however, that love of God and love of the world rested on the same premises. This realization influenced the troubadours' concept of love more than the sometimes too radical schema critics apply today speaking of Marcabru and his followers. Even less impression seems to have been made by the later triple division of love developed by the Scholastics. Thomas Aquinas differentiates: 1. divine love *(charitas);* 2. premeditated love *(dilectio),* determined by reason and the will; 3. sensual love *(amor).*

Although the troubadours often candidly allow their erotic desires to glimmer through, or even speak openly of them, many traits of similarity can be found with the mystics, which are in all probability direct copies. This is particularly true where it is less the person than the personification of love that is being glorified. As has already been mentioned, these two are often identical. A passage out of Sermon LXXIII of St. Bernard (quoted in Lot-Borodine) may illustrate why it is possible to speak of the theory of *l'art pour l'art* in connection with the vaguely mystical troubadours, especially as it complements the theory of *l'amour pour l'amour:* "Amo quia amo, ut amem." Not only the Bible but also Augustine reminds believers of the words of St. John: "Deus est charitas." For him, love is first of all a signal for absolute subjection, not for ecstatic rapture.

Another theme, that of the *mal d'aimer,* in which the troubadours anticipate the Romantics, is likewise of mystical origin. A commentator and continuator of Bernard, Abbé Gilbert de Hoy, once wrote: "Ubi viget amor, ibi vigit languor, si absit quod amatur" (quoted in Lot-Borodine). A closer examination of the mystical elements in the love lyrics would perhaps show that they are more closely related to speculative mysticism, such as that practised later (fourteenth century) by Meister Eckart, than to the decidedly affective mysticism of Bernard. In this connection, each poet would have to be examined independently.

A few examples have been chosen to illustrate what has just been discussed. In order to give expression to its feelings, the language of mysticism prefers extravagant words: "Burn, wound, intoxication, pierce, eternal imprisonment, martyrdom, cross, slave of pity," etc. belong to mystical vocabulary: Guillaume IX, *Farai chansoneta nueva* (ed. Jeanroy, VIII, 7-12, p. 20):

> Qu'ans mi *rent* a lieys e·m *liure,*
> Qu'en sa carta·m pot escriure.
> E no m'en tengatz per *yure*
> S'ieu ma bona dompna am,
> Quar senes lieys non puesc viure,
> Tant ai pres de s'amor *gran fam.*

(On the contrary I give myself to her, and deliver myself into her hands, so that she can note me down in her charter [perhaps a pun, with the double meaning: paper, and cardgame, that is, she can include me in her game, for she has many true suitors, as is declared in line 26]. And do not consider me a *drunkard,* if I love my good lady, for I cannot live without her, so *hungry* am I for her love.)

Bernard de Ventadour, *Per melhs cobrir lo mal pes e·l cossire* (ed. Lazar, 21, 7-12, p. 140):

> Anc Deus no fetz *trebalha* ni *martire*
> Ses mal d'amor, qu'eu no *sofris* en patz;
> Mas d'aquel sui, si be·m peza, *sofrire,*
> C'Amors mi fai amar lai on li platz;
> E dic vos be que s'eu no sui amatz,
> Ges no reman en la mia nualha.

(Never did God create any torment or agony which I do not suffer in peace, save the pain of love. But I endure it, though it is difficult for me, since Love makes me love where it pleases him. I assure you that if I am not loved, it is not the fault of my indolence.)

Peire Vidal praises love as he would God: *Be m'agrada la covinens sazos* (ed. Anglade, XXVII, 9-16, p. 86):

> Amors mi te jauzent e deleitos,
> Amors mi ten en son dous recaliu,
> Amors mi te galhart e esforsiu;
> Per amor sui pensiu se consiros;
> Per amor sui tan fort enamoratz,
> Que d'amor son totas mas volontatz,
> Per amor em cortezi' e joven,
> Quar d'amor son mei fag e mei parven.

(Love makes me happy and cheerful, love keeps me in its sweet heat, love keeps me vigorous and brave, through love I am pensive and musing; thanks to love I am so enamoured, that all my wishes are of love; thanks to love I like courtesy and youth, for all my actions and my behaviour are generated by love.)

The martyrdom of love and infinite patience are often mentioned in Bernard de Ventadour's poems, as in the *tornada* of *Tant ai mo cor ple de joya* (ed. Lazar, 4, 73-76, p. 76):

> Messatgers; vai e cor,
> E di·m a la gensor
> La *pena* e la *dolor*
> Que·n trac, e·l martire.

(Go, messenger, run and speak for me; tell the fairest lady of the pain, the grief and the torment which I suffer for her.)

The extravagances lies here not only in the words but also in their accumulation.

The ecstatic surge of happiness at the thought of the lady corresponds to the feeling of the mystics as they describe the nearness of God. The tone is exaggerated, as in the hymns: Peire Vidal, *Be m'agrada la covinens sazos* (ed. Anglade, XXVII, 17-24, p. 87):

> Bel m'es, bela domna, quan pens de vos
> E bel quar sui en vostre senhoriu,
> Bel m'es quan n'aug bon pretz nominatiu,
> E bel quan vei vostras belas faissos.
> Bel m'es quan gart vostras finas beutatz
> E bel quar sui tot vostr'endomenjatz,
> Bel m'es quar ai en vos mon pensamen
> E bel quar am vos sola solamen.

(I am happy, beautiful lady, when I think of you, happy because I am under your command, happy when I hear word of your merit and happy when I see your splendid appearance. I am happy when I contemplate your perfect beauty, happy because I am your loyal subject, I am happy because my thoughts are directed toward you, and happy because I love you and you alone.)

Peire Vidal's happiness makes him lose his identity: *Be m'agrada la covinens sazos* (ed. Anglade, XXVII, 38-39, p. 88):

> Bona domna, tan fort m'apoderatz,
> Domna, que d'als non es ma volontatz;
>
> (Good lady, you have me so much in your power that my will has no other goal.)

Finally, mystical rapture is the object of a *canso* by Gaucelm Faidit, *Mon cor e mi*, II, 13: [40]

> C'aissi·m pasmei, quan vos vi dels huoills rire
> C'una doussors d'amor me vene *ferir*
> Al cor, qu·m fetz si tremblar e fremir
> C'a pauc denan vos mori de desire.
>
> (For I so lost control of myself when I saw your laughing eyes, that my heart was struck by the sweetness of love, which made me so tremble and shake I almost died of longing for your presence.)

Will power, self-control and self-determination all melt away at the sight of the beloved. For Pollmann, courtly love

> needs the physical element only in order to lay stress on its basically ecstatic conception. [...] One could allege for the defense of the ecstatic nature of the *fin'amors* that a real ecstasy, as Abelard demands it for the love of God, does not exist in the mystics either. There, too, it is a relative ecstasy, a 'love of God for God's sake,' which can never be separated from its consequence, i.e. the actual approaching of God through this love. That the troubadours of the *fin'amors* tried to emphasize the disinterestedness *[Selbstlosigkeit]* of their love as did the mystics with the love of God, and that they conceived of their love as an ecstatic one, cannot be questioned. [41]

The remarks concluding the preceeding chapter are also valid for this one. A good example for an ambivalent activity is worshipping: very close to praying, it has always been one of the favourite way of expressions of a lover addressing himself to the beloved. The relationship between mariology and poetry

---

[40] Quoted in Kolsen, *Studi Medievali*, XVI, 1943-50, p. 256.
[41] Pollmann, *op. cit.*, p. 158.

has been the topic of several special studies (cf. Ashmann, Scheludko et al.).

A basic notion which embraces practically all kinds of human relations is *authority*. Beginning with the authority exerted by leaders of primitive tribes, of the head of the family (be it now the father- or mother-type head), the authoritative principle as such became quickly institutionalized as one of the bases of social life. The political, legal and religious power — if they were not embodied by a single person or institution — needed and still need authority as a principle guaranteeing a certain order. It was St. Augustine's conception and definition of *autoritas* which prevailed during the High Middle Ages. Its feudal structure could not have been possible had the principle of authority as such been questioned. And when it was questioned, i.e. brought openly into relation with the principle of power, it did not disappear, it was only shifted to the man who could decret it because he was strong enough to do so. That the troubadours connected the dependency of the lover on the beloved with the dependency of the vassal on his master, adopting thereby the language and gestures of the feudal system, is quite natural. The troubadours never tired of putting forth the *oboedientia,* the absolute submission to the lady's authority, as a *conditio sine que non* for the qualification as a good lover.

There was, however, a point beyond which submissive behaviour became a pretext for the poetic creations of lovers and would-be-lovers. As the catalogue of the themes of *cortezia* tries to show, we detect in Old Provençal poetry the cultivated pleasure of playing with the transposition of different categories: the moral, the religious, the profane and the aesthetic become exchangeable values. This leads us to the final observation that the tendency towards the institution of a religion of love was the product of *meridional libertinage*. Needless to say, the implications of such a term necessitate a special investigation. At least we can define for the time being meridional libertinage as a skillful mixture of "savoir faire" and "sovoir vivre." Aesthetically, it was best expressed in the secular context of Old Provençal lyrics whose recourse to religious words and themes, more often than not served an ironic purpose.

IN LIEU OF A CONCLUSION

I think, as do Wettstein and Lazar,[1] that a religious interpretation of terms like *razo, mesura, sen,* often used synonymously, and even of *merce,* remains impossible whenever they are used in a love poem. It is the social, moral and aesthetic impact on the troubadour's conception of love, on one hand, and his spiritual and intellectual tradition, rooted in the Church and the society, on the other hand, which made the intermixture of the vocabulary of these two main fields of human activity possible. "Si rhétorique et casuistique il y a," says Lazar, concerning the *Fin'Amors,* "elles ne se trouvent pas dans les mots employés, mais dans l'essai de justifier moralement un amour amoral, voire même immoral, considéré du point de vue de l'Eglise."[2] It is precisely because of this moral justification, generated by the threat of the Church, that the vocabulary of the troubadours, dealing mainly with sinful love, i.e. adultery, glided more and more toward religious categories. The troubadours invented an aesthetic adjustment to a moral requirement. Finally, it cannot be overlooked that the *Fin'Amors* raised the status of the woman, psychologically as well as socially. Conjugal love made of her a sort of prisoner of her husband who possessed her physically and by contract of marriage. He did not have to court her in order to obtain what he wanted. The lover, however, paid not only court to his *midons,* but, doubly threatened by the jealous husband and the finger raising Church, he created a *moral alibi* through the poetic

---

[1] Wettstein, Jacques, *"Mezura." L'idéal des troubadours; son essence et ses aspects,* dissertation, Zurich, 1945, p. 35; Lazar, Moshé, *op. cit.,* p. 31.
[2] *Ibid.,* p. 57.

expression of his suffering and worship. Out of this artistic game, then, out of a highly ambiguous situation which he obviously enjoyed, arose the equally ambiguous secular lyrics adorned with religious elements.

A SELECTIVE BIBLIOGRAPHY [1]

ASHMANN, M. *Le culte de la Sainte Vierge et la littérature profane du moyen âge*, Utrecht, 1930.
ALONSO, D. "Cancioncillas de amigos mozárabes. Primavera temprana de la lírica europea," *Revista de Filología Española*, XXIII, 1950, pp. 297-349.
ANGLADE, J. *Les Troubadours, leurs vies, leurs œuvres, leur influence*, Paris[4], 1929.
AUERBACH, E. "Passio als Leidenschaft," *PMLA*, LV, 1941, pp. 1179-96.
"Typologische Motive in der mittelalterlichen Literatur," *Schriften und Vorträge des Petrarca-Institutes*, Köln, II, 1953.
AVALLE D'ARCO, S. *La letteratura medievale in lingua d'oc nella sua tradizione manoscritta*, Turin, 1961.
AXHAUSEN, K. *Die Theorien über den Ursprung der provenzalischen Lyrik*, dissertation, Marburg, 1937.
BARTSCH, K. *Grundriss zur Geschichte der provenzalischen Literatur*, Elberfeld, 1872.
BATTAGLIA, S. *I primi trovatori*, Naples, 1940.
"Introduzione alla lirica dei trovatori," *Romana*, V, 1941, pp. 409-423.
La lirica medioevale, Naples, 1956.
BECKER, PH. A. "Vom geistlichen Tagelied," *Volkstum und Kultur der Romanen*, II, 1929, pp. 293-302.
"Vom christlichen Hymnus zum Minnesang," *Historisches Jahrbuch der Görresgesellschaft*, LII, 1932, pp. 1-39 and 145-177.
BELPERRON, P. *La Croisade contre les Albigeois et l'union du Languedoc à la France* (1209-1249), Paris, 1942.
La Joie d'Amour. Contribution à l'étude des Troubadours et de l'amour courtois, Paris, 1948.
BERTONI, G. "Le origini delle letterature romanze nel pensiero dei Romantici tedeschi," *Archivum Romanicum*, XIII, 1939, pp. 1-10.
BEZZOLA, R. R. "Guillaume IX et les origines de l'amour courtois," *Romania*, LXVI, 1940-41, pp. 145-237.
Les origines et la formation de la littérature courtoise en occident, 3 vol. Paris, 1944, 1958, 1960.
BOUTIERE, J. and SCHUTZ, A. H. *Biographie des troubadours*, Toulose-Paris, 1950.
BRIFFAULT, R. *Les troubadours et le sentiment romanesque*, Paris, 1954; rev. English version: *The Troubadours*, Bloomington, 1965.

---

[1] Contains only material pertaining to the subject and no editions.

BRINKMANN, H. *Entstehungsgeschichte des Minnesangs*, Halle, 1926.
CAMPROUX, C. *Histoire de la littérature occitane*, Paris, 1953.
"La Joie civilisatrice chez les troubadours," *La Table Ronde*, XCVII, January 1956, pp. 64-69.
"A propos de joi," *Mélanges de linguistique et de littérature romanes à la mémoire d'Istvàn Frank*, Annales Universitatis Saraviensis, VI, 1957, pp. 100-107.
La 'Joy d'Amor' des Troubadours. Jeu et joie d'amour, Montpellier, 1965.
CASELLA, M. *Poesia e Storia*. Archivio Storico Italiano, XCVI, 1938.
CASSOU, J. "Le message spirituel des troubadours," *Annales de l'Institut d'Etudes Occitanes*, I, Toulouse, 1948-49, pp. 115-120.
CHAILLEY, J. "Les premiers troubadours et les versus de l'école d'Aquitaine," *Romania*, LXXVI, 1955, p. 212.
"Notes sur les troubadours," *Mélanges de linguistique et de littérature romanes à la mémoire d'Istvàn Frank*, pp. 118-128.
CHAMBERS, F. M. "Imitation of Form in the Old Provençal Lyric," *Romance Philology*, VI, 1952-53, pp. 104-120.
CHAYTOR, H. J. *The Troubadours*, Cambridge, 1912.
CLUZEL, I. M. "Jaufré Rudel et l'Amor de lonh," *Romania*, LXXVIII, 1957, pp. 86-97.
"A propos des origines de la littérature courtoise en Occident," *Romania*, LXXXI, 1960, pp. 538-555.
"Les 'jaryas' et l'amour courtois," *Cultura Neolatina*, XX, 1960, pp. 233-248.
"Les plus anciens troubadours et la 'fin'amor,'" *Revue de Langue et Littérature Provençales*, III, 1960, pp. 26-43.
"Quelques réflexions à propos des origines de la poésie lyrique des troubadours," *Cahiers de Civilisation Médiévale*, IV, 1961, pp. 179-188.
"L'état présent des études relatives à l'ancienne littérature provençale," *Actes du VIIIe Congrès de l'Association Guillaume Budé*, Paris, 1964, pp. 435-445.
COHEN, G. "Les problèmes des origines arabes de la poésie provençale médiévale," *Bulletin de Belgique*, XXXII, Bruxelles, 1946, pp. 266-278.
Tableau de la littérature française médiévale, Idées et Sensibilités, Paris, 1950.
La grande clarté du moyen âge, Paris, 1945.
CONTINI, G. Review of Errante, *Belfagor*, IV, pp. 614-615.
CRESCINI, V. "I trovatori provenzali e la chiesa," *Conversazione della Domenica*, IV, No. 15, 1889.
Manuale per l'avviamento agli Studi provenzali, Milano[3], 1926.
CURTIUS, E. R. *Europäische Literatur und lateinisches Mittelalter*, Berne[3], 1961.
DAVENSON, H. *Les Troubadours*, Paris, 1961.
DÉFOURNEAUX, M. *Les Français en Espagne aux XIe et XIIe siècles*, Paris, 1949.
DENOMY, A. J. "An Inquiry into the Origins of Courtly Love," *Mediaeval Studies*, VI, 1944, pp. 246-256.
"*Fin'Amors*: The Pure Love of the Troubadours, Its Amorality and Possible Source," *Mediaeval Studies*, VII, 1945, pp. 139-207.
The Heresy of Courtly Love, Boston, 1947.

"*Jovens:* The Notion of Youth among the Troubadours, Its Meaning and Source," *Mediaeval Studies*, XI, 1949, pp. 1-22.
"*Jois* among the Early Troubadours, Its Meaning and Possible Source," *Mediaeval Studies*, XIII, 1951, pp. 177-217.
"Courtly Love and Courtliness," *Speculum*, XXVIII, 1953, pp. 44-63.
"Concerning the Accessibility of Arabic Influences to the Earliest Provençal Troubadours," *Mediaeval Studies*, XV, 1953, pp. 147-158.

DERMENGHEM, E. "Les grands thèmes de la poésie amoureuse chez les Arabes précurseurs des poètes d'oc," *Les Cahiers du Sud*, numéro spécial: *Le Génie d'oc et l'homme méditerranéen*, 1943, pp. 26 sq.

DIEZ, F. *Die Poesie der Troubadours*, Leipzig^2, 1883.
Leben und Werke der Troubadours, Leipzig^2, 1882.

DIONYSIUS AREOPAGITA. *On the Divine Names and the Mystical Theology*, transl. by C. E. Rolt, London, 1920.

DRONKE, P. "Guillaume IX and Courtoisie," *Romanische Forschungen*, LXXIII, 1961, pp. 327-338.
Medieval Latin and the Rise of European Love-Lyric, 2 vol., Oxford, 1965.

DUPIN, H. *La Courtoisie au Moyen Age*, Paris, 1931.

ECKER, L. *Arabischer, provenzalischer und deutscher Minnesang*, dissertation, Berne, 1934.

EL FASI, M. "La poésie arabe andalouse et son influence sur les troubadours provençaux," *Cahiers du Sud*, special issue, 1943, pp. 39 sq.

ERCKMANN, R. "Der Einfluss der arabisch-spanischen Kultur auf die Entwicklung des Minnesangs," *Deutsche Vierteljahresschrift*, IX, 1931, pp. 240-284.

ERRANTE, G. *Sulla lirica romanza delle origini*, New York, 1943.
"Old Provençal Poetry: Latin and Arabic Influences," *Thought*, XX, 1945, pp. 291-304.
Marcabru e le fonti sacre dell'antica lirica romanza, Florence, 1948.

FARAL, E. *Les Arts Poétiques du XIIe et du XIIIe siècle; Recherches et Documents sur la technique littéraire du Moyen Age*, Paris, 1924.

FEUERLICHT, I. "Vom Ursprung der Minne," *Archivum Romanicum*, XIII, 1939, pp. 140-177.

FRANK, G. "The distant love of Jaufré Rudel," *Modern Language Notes*, LVII, 1942, pp. 528-534.

FRANK, I. "Les débuts de la poésie courtoise en Catalogne et le problème des origines lyriques," *Actas y Memorias del VII° Congreso Internacional de Lingüística Románica*, Barcelona, 1955, pp. 972 sq.

FRAPPIER, J. *La poésie lyrique en France aux XIIe et XIIIe siècles; I: Les genres, II: Les auteurs*, Paris (C.D.U.), 1949.
"Vues sur les conceptions courtoises dans les littératures d'oc et d'oïl du XIIe siècle," *Cahiers de Civilisation Médiévale*, II, 1959, pp. 135-156.

FRINGS, T. *Minnesänger und Troubadours*, Berlin, 1949.

FURSTNER, H. *Studien zur Wesensbestimmung der höfischen Minne*, Groningen, 1956.

GABRIELI, F. "La Poesia arabe e le letterature occidentali," *Belfagor*, IX, 1954, pp. 377-386 and 510-520.

GALPIN, M. S. *Cortois and Vilain: A Study of the Distinction Made between Them by the French and Provençal Poets of the 12th, 13th and 14th Century*, New Haven, 1905.

GARCÍA GÓMEZ, E. "La lírica hispano-árabe y la aparición de la lírica románica," *Al Andalus*, XXI, 1956, pp. 303-333.

GENNRICH, F. "Zur Ursprungsfrage des Minnesangs," *Deutsche Vierteljahresschrift*, VII, 1929, pp. 187-228.

"Das Formproblem des Minnesangs. Ein Beitrag zur Erforschung des Strophenbaus der mittelalterlichen Lyrik," *Deutsche Vierteljahresschrift*, IX, 1931, pp. 285 sq.

"Grundsätzliches zu den Troubadour- und Trouvèreweisen," *Zeitschrift für Romanische Philologie*, LVII, 1937, pp. 31-56.

GIBB, H. "The Influence of Islamic Culture on Medieval Europe," *Bulletin of the John Rylands Library* (Manchester), 1955, pp. 82-98.

GILSON, E. *Les idées et les lettres, Essais d'art et de philosophie*, Paris, 1932², 1955.

La Théologie mystique de Saint Bernard, Paris, 1934; cf. app. IV: "St. Bernard et l'amour courtois," pp. 193-216.

L'Ecole des Muses, Essais d'art et de philosophie, Paris, 1951.

La Philosophie au Moyen Age, Paris², 1952.

HATZFELD, H. Review of Denomy's *The Heresy of Courtly Love*, *Symposium*, II, No. 2, November 1948, pp. 285-288.

HEINIMANN, S. "*Dulcis*," *Homenaje a Dámaso Alonso*, Madrid, 1961, pp. 215-32.

Das Abstraktum in der französischen Literatursprache des Mittelalters, series *Romanica Helvetica*, No. 73, 1963.

HOEPFFNER, E. *Les Troubadours, dans leur vie et dans leurs œuvres*, Paris, 1955.

IMBS, P. *Bilan d'une poésie: la lyrique des troubadours* (Review-article of Hoepffner's book), *Annali della Scuola Normale Superiore di Pisa*, II, vol. XXV, 1956, pp. 106-123.

"A la recherche d'une littérature cathare," *Revue du moyen âge latin*, V, 1949, pp. 289-302.

JANSSEN, H. "Quelques remarques sur les rapports entre l'ancienne poésie provençale et les Hymnes de l'Eglise," *Neophilologus*, XVIII, 1933, pp. 262-271.

JEANROY, A. *Les origines de la poésie lyrique en France au moyen âge*, Paris³, 1925.

"La première génération des troubadours," *Romania*, LVI, 1930, pp. 487-525.

"Les études provençales du XVIe siècle au milieu du XIXe siècle," *Annales du Midi*, XLIII, 1931, pp. 129-159.

La poésie lyrique des Troubadours, 2 vol., Paris, 1934.

JODOGNE, O. "Encore sur l'origine arabe de la poésie provençale," *Les lettres romanes*, IV, 1950, pp. 237-238.

KELLY, A. "Eleanor of Aquitaine and her courts of love," *Speculum*, XII, 1937, pp. 3-19.

Eleanor of Aquitaine and the Four Kings, Cambridge, Mass., 1951.

KINKEL, H. " Die kulturellen Grundlagen der provenzalischen Trobadordichtung," *Archiv für das Studium der neueren Sprachen und Literaturen*, CXXII, 1909, pp. 332-345.

KNINGS, H. *Die Geschichte des Wortschatzes der Höflichkeit im Französischen*, Bonn, 1961.

KÖHLER, E. "Zum *trobar clus* der Trobadors," *Romanische Forschungen*, LXIV, 1925, pp. 71-101.

"Reichtum und Freigebigkeit in der Trobadordichtung," *Estudis Romànics*, III, 1951-52, pp. 103-138.
"Scholastische Aesthetik und höfische Dichtung," *Neophilologus*, XXXVII, 1953, pp. 202-207.
Trobadorlyrik und höfischer Roman, Berlin, 1962.
"No sai qui s'es...," *Mélanges de Linguistique Romane et de Philologie Médiévale, offerts à M. Maurice Delbouille*, II, 1964, pp. 349-366.
"Observations historiques et sociologiques sur la poésie des troubadours," *Cahiers de Civilisation Médiévale*, VII, 1964, pp. 27-51.
KOLSEN, A. *Dichtungen der Trobadors*, Halle, 1916-19.
Beiträge zur altprovenzalischen Lyrik, Florence, 1939.
KRÜGER, P. *Bedeutung und Entwicklung der "salutatio,"* dissertation, Greifswald, 1912.
LAPA, R. "As origens líricas. Estado actual do problema," *Boletim de filogia*, I, 1932-33, pp. 8-32.
LAFITTE-HOUSSAT, J. *Troubadours et Cours d'Amor*, Paris, 1950.
LAZAR, M. *L'idéologie et la casuistique de l'amour courtois dans la littérature du XIIe siècle*, Paris, 1957.
Amour courtois et "fin'amors" dans la littérature du XIIe siècle, Paris, 1964.
LE GENTIL, P. *Le "Virelai" et le "Villancico"; le problème des origines arabes*, Paris, 1954.
LEJEUNE, R. "Rôle littéraire d'Aliénor d'Aquitaine et de sa famille," *Cultura Neolatina*, XIV, 1954, pp. 5-57.
"Formules féodales et style amoureux chez Guillaume IX d'Aquitaine," *VIII° Congresso di Studi romanzi*, Florence, 1956, pp. 227-248.
"Rôle littéraire de la famille d'Aliénor d'Aquitaine," *Cahiers de Civilisation Médiévale*, I, 1958, pp. 319-337.
"La chanson de 'l'amour de loin' de Jaufré Rudel," *Studi in onore di Angelo Monteverdi*, I, 1959, pp. 403-442.
LERCH, E. "Trobadorsprache und religiöse Sprache," *Cultura Neolatina*, III, 1943, pp. 214-230.
LÉVI-PROVENÇAL, E. *Poésie arabe d'Espagne et poésie d'Europe médiévale*, Paris, 1948.
"Les vers arabes de la chanson V de Guillaume IX d'Aquitaine," *Arabica*, I, 1954, pp. 208-211.
LEWIS, C. S. *The allegory of love*, New York, 1958.
LI GOTTI, E. "La 'Tesi Araba' sulle 'Origini' della Lirica romanza," *Studi Medievali in onore di Antonio di Stefano*, Palermo, 1956, pp. 294-339.
DE LOLLIS, C. *Poesie provenzali sulla genesi d'amore*, Rome, 1927.
LOMMATZSCH, E. *Leben und Lieder der provenzalischen Troubadours*, 2 vol., Berlin, 1957-59.
LOT-BORODINE, M. "Sur les origines et les fins du 'service d'amour provençal,'" *Mélanges de linguistique et de littérature offerts à M. Alfred Jeanroy*, Paris, 1928, pp. 223-242.
De l'amour profane à l'amour sacré, Paris, 1961. (Contains, among others, the same article mentioned above. Cf. pp. 71-88.)
LOWINSKY, V. "Zum geistlichen Kunstlied in der altprovenzalischen Literatur," *Zeitschrift für französische Sprache und Literatur*, XX, 1898, pp. 163 sq.
MENÉNDEZ PIDAL, R. "Poesía árabe y poesía europea," *Bulletin Hispanique*, XL, 1938, pp. 337-423.

"La primitiva lírica europea," *Revista de Filología Española*, XLIII, 1960, pp. 279-354.

MERK, C. J. *Anschauungen über die Lehre und das Leben der Kirche im altfranzösischen Heldenopos*, Beiheft No. 41 of the *Zeitschrift für Romanische Philologie*, Halle, 1918.

METTMANN, W. "Zur Diskussion über die literaturgeschichtliche Bedeutung der mozarabischen Jarchas," *Romanische Forschungen*, LXX, 1958, pp. 1-29.

MILLÁS VALLICROSA, J. M. *La poesía sagrada hebraico-española*, Madrid², 1948.

MOLDENHAUER, G. Introducción a la primitiva poesía provenzal," *Humanitas*, II, 1959, pp. 147-166.

MOLLER, H. "The Meaning of Courtly Love," *Journal for American Folklore*, LXXIII, 1960, pp. 39-52.

MONFRIN, J. "Travaux relatifs à l'ancien français et à l'ancien provençal parus en France de 1940-1945," *Le Moyen Age*, LIV, 1948, pp. 327-357 and *ibid.*, LV, 1949, pp. 127-156.

MOORE, O. H. "Jaufré Rudel and the Lady of Dreams," *PMLA*, XXIX, 1914, pp. 517-536.

MORERE, M. "Les données historiques de l'influence de la poésie andalouse sur la lyrique des Troubadours," *Annales de l'Institut d'Etudes Occitanes*, Toulouse, 1951, pp. 48-60.

MULERTT, W. "Über die Frage nach der Herkunft der Trobadorkunst," *Neuphilologische Mitteilungen*, XXII, 1921, p. 1 sq.

NELLI, R. "De l'amour provençal," *Revue de Synthèse*, LXIV, 1948, pp. 15 sq.
"Du catharisme à l'amour provençal," *ibid.*, pp. 31 sq.
"La fin de l'amour provençal," *La Table Ronde*, XCVII, 1956, pp. 70-81.
"Sur l'amour provençal," *Cahiers du Sud*, XLVII, 1958, pp. 3-37.
L'érotique des Troubadours, Contribution éthno-sociologiques à l'étude des origines sociales du sentiment et de l'idée d'amour, Toulouse, 1963.

NYKL, A. R. *Dove's Neck Ring about Love and Lovers*, Paris, 1931.
"The Latest in Troubadour Studies," *Archivum Romanicum*, XIX, 1935, pp. 227-236.
"L'influence arabe-andalouse sur les troubadours," *Bulletin Hispanique*, XLI, 1939, pp. 305-315.
Troubadour Studies: a Critical Survey of Recent Books Published in this Field, Cambridge, Mass., 1944.
Hispano-Arabic Poetry and Its Relations with the Old Provençal Troubadours, Baltimore, 1946.

PELLEGRINI, S. "Intorno al vassallagio d'amore dei primi trovatori," *Cultura Neolatina*, IV-V, 1944-45, pp. 21-36.

PÉRES, H. *La Poésie andalouse en arabe classique au XIe siècle*, Paris, 1937.
"La poésie arabe de l'Andalousie et ses relations possibles avec la poésie des troubadours," *Cahiers du Sud*, special issue: *L'Islam et l'Occident*, 1947, pp. 107-130.

PILLET, A. *Zum Ursprung der altprovenzalischen Lyrik*, Halle, 1928.

PILLET, A. and CARSTENS, H. *Bibliographie der Troubadours*, Halle, 1933 sq.

PITANGUE, F. *Les troubadours furent-ils les missionnaires de l'albigéisme?* Toulouse, 1946.

POLLMANN, L. "Dichtung und Liebe bei Wilhelm von Aquitanien," *Zeitschrift für Romanische Philologie*, LXXVIII, 1962, pp. 326-357.

"*Joie e solatz*, zur Geschichte einer Begriffskontamination," *Zeitschrift für Romanische Philologie*, LXXX, 1964, pp. 256-286.
"*Trobar clus*," *Bibelexegese und hispano-arabische Literatur*, Münster, 1965.
Die Liebe in der hochmittelalterlichen Literatur Frankreichs, Versuch einer historischen Phänomenologie, Frankfurt, 1966.
PUCCI-LAVY, C. "Le 'Corti d'amore,'" *Quaderni Ibero-Americani*, II, No. 10, 1951, pp. 53-55.
RÉMY, P. "Les 'Cours d'Amour,' légende et réalité," *Revue de l'université de Bruxelles*, VII, 1954-55, pp. 1-9.
RIBERA, J. *La música andaluza medieval en las canciones de Trovadores, Troveros y Minnesinger*, Madrid, 1923-25.
DE RIQUER, M. *La Lírica de los Trovadores*, Barcelona, 1948.
ROBERTSON, D. W. "Amors de terra lonhdana," *Studies in Philology*, XLIX, 1952, pp. 566-582.
"The Subject of the *De Amore* of Andreas Capellanus," *Modern Philology*, L, 1952-53, pp. 145-161.
ROHLFS, G. *Romanische Philologie*, vol. I: *Französische und provenzalische Philologie*, Heidelberg, 1950.
ROHR, R. "Zur Skala der ritterlichen Tugenden in der altprovenzalischen und altfranzösischen Dichtung," *Zeitschrift für Romanische Philologie*, LXXVIII, 1962, pp. 292-326.
ROLAND-MANUEL "La musique et l'amour courtois," *La Table Ronde*, XCVII, 1956, pp. 82-83.
RONCAGLIA, A. Review of Errante's book, *Cultura Neolatina*, IX, 1949, pp. 183-191.
ROSENBERG, M. V. *Eleanor of Aquitaine, Queen of the Troubadours and of the Courts of Love*, Boston, 1937.
SALVERDA DE GRAVE, J. J. "Quelques observations sur les origines de la poésie des troubadours," *Neophilologus*, III, 1918, pp. 247-252.
"Observations sur l'art lyrique de Giraut de Borneil," *Mededeelingen kkl. nederl. Akad. v. Wetensch. Afd. Letterkunde* I, I, Amsterdam, 1938, pp. 79 sq.
SANTANGELO, S. "L'amore lontano di Jaufre Rudel," *Siculorum Gymnasium*, VI, 1953, pp. 1-28.
SCHELUDKO, D. "Über die arabischen Lehnwörter im Altprovenzalischen," *Zeitschrift für Romanische Philologie*, XLVII, 1927, pp. 418-442.
"Beiträge zur Entstehungsgeschichte der altprovenzalischen Lyrik," *Archivum Romanicum*, XI, 1927, pp. 273-312; *ibid.*, XII, 1928, pp. 30-127; *ibid.*, XV, 1931, pp. 137-206; *Zeitschrift für französische Sprache und Literatur*, LII, 1929, pp. 1-38 and pp. 201-66.
"Ovid und die Trobadors," *Zeitschrift für französische Sprache und Literatur*, LIV, 1934, pp. 129-174.
"Über den Frauenkult der Trobadors," *Neuphilologische Mitteilungen*, XXXV, 1934, pp. 140.
"Die Marienlieder in der altprovenzalischen Lyrik," *Neuphilologische Mitteilungen*, XXXVI, 1935, pp. 29-48.
"Religiöse Elemente im weltlichen Liebeslied der Trobadors," *Zeitschrift für französische Sprache und Literatur*, LIX, 1935, pp. 402-421; *ibid.*, LX, 1937, pp. 18-35.
"Über die religiöse Lyrik der Trobadors," *Neuphilologische Mitteilungen*, XXXVIII, 1937, pp. 224-250.

"Über die Theorien der Liebe bei den Trobadors," *Zeitschrift für Romanische Philologie*, LX, 1940, pp. 191-234.
SCHLÖSSER, F. *Andreas Capellanus: seine Minnelehre und das christliche Weltbild um 1200*, dissertation, Bonn, 1960.
SCHRÖTTER, W. *Ovid und die Troubadours*, Halle, 1908.
SCHUTZ, A. H. "The Provençal Expression *pretz e valor*," *Speculum*, XIX, 1944, pp. 488-493.
SETTEGAST, F. "Über *joi* in der Sprache der Trobadors," *Berichte über die Verhandlungen der Königlichen Sächsischen Gesellschaft der Wissenschaften*, vol. 41, 1889, pp. 99 sq.
SINGER, S. "Arabische und europäische Poesie im Mittelalter," *Zeitschrift für deutsche Philologie*, LII, 1927, pp. 77-92.
SPANKE, H. "Die Theorien Riberas über Zusammenhänge zwischen frühromanischer Strophenform und andalusisch-arabischer Lyrik des Mittelalters," *Volkstum und Kultur der Romanen*, III, 1930, pp. 258-278.
"Zur Formenkunst der ältesten Troubadours," *Studi Medievali*, VII, 1934, pp. 72-84.
Beziehungen zwischen romanischer und mittellateinischer Lyrik mit besonderer Berücksischtigung der Metrik und Musik, Berlin, 1936.
"Die Ursprünge des romanischen Minnesangs," *Geistige Arbeit*, VII, 1940, pp. 5-6.
Untersuchungen über die Ursprünge des romanischen Minnesangs, Göttingen, 1940.
"La teoría árabe sobre el origen de la lírica románica a la luz de las últimas investigaciones," *Anuario Musical*, I, 1946, pp. 5-18.
SPITZER, L. *L'Amour lointain de Jaufré Rudel et le sens de la poésie des troubadours*, Chapel Hill, 1944; *Romanische Literaturstudien*, Tübingen, 1959, which contains the same study, pp. 363-421.
Review of Santangelo's book, *Romania*, LXXV, 1954, pp. 396-402.
Review of Lot-Borodine, *Romanische Literaturstudien*, 1959.
SPÖRRI, TH. "Wilhelm von Poitiers und die Anfänge der abendländischen Poesie," *Trivium*, II, 1944, pp. 255-277.
STEGER, H. A. *Askese und 'Amour courtois.' Ein Beitrag zur Ortsbestimmung der altprovenzalischen Literatur*, dissertation, Heidelberg, 1933.
STÖSSEL, CH. *Bilder und Vergleiche in der provenzalischen Lyrik*, dissertation, Marburg, 1886.
STOROST, J. "Die Kunst der provenzalischen Trobadors," *Deutsches Dante-Jahrbuch*, XXV/XXVI, 1957, pp. 136-152.
STRONSKI, S. *Poésie et réalité aux temps des Troubadours*, Oxford, 1943.
VECCHI, G. "Il problema delle origini nella lirica romanza. Cospiranti conferme letterarie e musicologiche di una teoria," *Convivium*, 1949, fasc. VI.
VISCARDI, A. "La tradizione aulica e scolastica e la poesia trobadorica," *Studi Medievali*, VII, 1934, pp. 151-164.
"Intorno al problema delle origini trobadoriche," *Atti del Istituto Veneto di scienze, lettere ed arti*, 1933-34, VII, pp. 151 sq.
Storia della letteratura d'oc e d'oïl, Milano, 1959.
"Le origini della letteratura cortese," *Zeitschrift für Romanische Philologie*, LXXVIII, 1962, pp. 269-291.
"Le origine romanze e la tradizione letteraria mediolatina," *Mélanges... Delbouille*, II, Gembloux, 1964, pp. 687-704.

VOSSLER, K. "Die Kunst des ältesten Trobadors," *Miscellanea di Studi in onore di Attilio Hortis*, Triest, 1910, pp. 419 sq.
"Die Dichtung der Trobadors und ihre europäische Wirkung," *Romanische Forschungen*, LI, 1937, pp. 253 sq.
Die Dichtungsformen der Romanen, ed. by A. Bauer, Stuttgart, 1951.
WARREN, F. M. "The Romance Lyric from the Standpoint of Antecedent Latin Documents," *PMLA*, 1911, pp. 280-314.
WECHSSLER, E. *Das Kulturproblem des Minnesangs*, Halle, 1909.
WERNER, E. "Zur Frauenfrage und zum Frauenkult im Mittelater: Robert von Abrissel und Fontevrault," *Forschungen und Fortschritte*, XIX, 1955, pp. 269-276.
WETTSTEIN, J. "*Mezura*," *L'Idéal des troubadours, son essence et ses aspects*, dissertation, Zurich, 1945.
WILCOX, J. "Defining Courtly Love," *Michigan Academy of Sciences, Arts and Literature*, XII, 1930, pp. 313-325.
WINKLER, M. *Der kirchliche Wortschatz in der Epik Chrétien von Troyes*, dissertation, Munich, 1958.
ZORZI, D. *Valori religiosi nella letteratura provenzale. La spiritualità trinitaria*, Milano, 1954.
"*L'amor de lonh* di Jaufre Rudel," *Aevum*, XXIX, 1955, pp. 124-144.
ZUMTHOR, P. "Au berceau du lyrisme européen," *Cahiers du Sud*, XL, 1954, pp. 3 sq.
"Recherches sur les topiques dans la poésie lyrique des XIIe et XIIIe siècles," *Cahiers de Civilisation Médiévale*, II, 1959, pp. 409-427.

Having finished our study we received a new anthology of outstanding articles. Those dealing with our topic are included in the selective bibliography:
BAEHR, R. (ed.) *Der provenzalische Minnesang. Ein Querschnitt durch die neuere Forschungskiskussion*, Darmstadt, 1967. (Authors are: Storost, Pillet, Rohr, Gennrich, Spanke, Spoerri, Spitzer, Roncaglia, Feuerlicht, Scheludko, Silverstein, Köhler, Lerch, Vossler, Frank.)

www.ingramcontent.com/pod-product-compliance
Lightning Source LLC
Chambersburg PA
CBHW020421230426
43663CB00007BA/1257